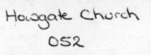

The Bloke's Bible

The Bloke's Bible

Dave Hopwood

Authentic

LONDON • COLORADO SPRINGS • HYDERABAD

13 12 11 10 09 08 07   9 8 7 6 5 4 3
Reprinted 2006, 2007
First published 2006 by Authentic Media
9 Holdom Avenue, Bletchley, Milton Keynes, MK1 1QR, UK
1820 Jet Stream Drive, Colorado Springs, CO 80921, USA
OM Authentic Media, Medchal Road, Jeedimetla Village,
Secunderabad 500 055, A.P., India
www.authenticmedia.co.uk

Authentic Media is a division of IBS-STL U.K., limited by guarantee, with
its Registered Office at Kingstown Broadway, Carlisle, Cumbria CA3 0HA.
Registered in England & Wales No. 1216232. Registered charity 270162)

British Library Cataloguing in Publication Data
A catalogue record for this book is available from the British Library

ISBN-13: 978-1-85078-712-9
ISBN-10: 1-85078-712-3

Cover Design by Sam Redwood
Print Management by Adare Carwin
Printed in Great Britain by J.H. Haynes & Co., Sparkford

Contents

Dedication		vii
Foreword		ix
Introduction		xiii

1.	Bathsheba's Bath	1
2.	Ehud's a Hood	9
3.	Job's Got Boils	16
4.	The Man Who Would Be King	24
5.	Adam's Best Mate	36
6.	Born to Be Wild	44
7.	The Horror, the Horror	53
8.	Peter Peter's Out	60
9.	No Bull Thomas	68
10.	Castration and Crucifixion	76
11.	The Glittering Cage	83
12.	How to Be a Shiny, Happy Person	89
13.	Red, Red Wine	95
14.	Death Wish	104
15.	Proud and Prejudiced	113
16.	Getting Tooled Up	119
17.	You Can Choose Your Friends . . .	125
18.	Moses the Murderer	134
19.	Cross-carrying for Beginners	142
20.	Enduring Little Children	149

21. It's Not All Work, Work, Work   156
22. Sin City   163
23. Show Me the Money   170
24. Talking from Balaam's Ass   178
25. The Evil That Men Do   186
26. The Creator and the Call Girl   196
27. Ezekiel's Dung   204
28. Party On   209

Dedication

For my beautiful Lynn (who copes brilliantly with
two children in our house),
and Amy, our gorgeous Exocet missile.
And for Justin, my very good friend: thanks for
keeping me sane and laughing.
Without you guys this book would never have been
written.

Foreword

We men are our own worst enemy. We know we're fragile inside, even if we keep up the tough appearance. We know that we're weak, even if we like to look strong.

And so we participate in a conspiracy of silent grunts and nods and poses that are meant to say BACK OFF: everything's cool, it's sorted, it's sussed. No matter if I'm grieving the death of my mum, or you're crippled with jealousy or he's – whisper it – just really lonely.

It's OK. It's OK. Isn't it?

Hang on. Who said we needed to play this game in the first place? Jesus didn't. In fact, he said he'd come to turn this whole stupid world upside down, inside out. The first will be last. The weak ones are strong. The poor are rich.

Except, of course, that it's hard not to play the game, even if we follow Jesus. We don't always get it. We like to be strong leaders, because that's what men do best: tell others what to do. We forget that the best leaders serve by washing feet . . .

We strap on our public face of Christian goodness, our whiter-than-white mask of holiness that dazzles and distracts you from the fact that most 'strong' men can talk a great talk but can't always walk the walk.

We fail. We falter. We fall. It's OK. It's OK. It's OK.

Dave Hopwood's honestly observed book is a sigh of relief. It looks you in the eye and says: 'Wait a minute. Pull up a stool. Sit down. Let me buy you a drink, for God's sake . . . and for yours. Talk to me. We might just find that we have something in common. It's OK…'

It's OK for men to cry inside. It's OK for men to wonder why they're here, where they're going, why they're so hung up. It's OK. Nothing is new: it's all been done before. That amazing king David, who wrote those beautiful psalms to God – he messed up. He had feelings, just like me, that got him into trouble. Got a man killed, even. He could help himself, but he chose not to. Sound familiar?

So, Dave watches the world from his local, Cutter's, where he also turns to his bruised and battered Bible for solace and wisdom. It's a kind of 'double listening' – listening sympathetically to the world, and carefully to the Word – so that both can begin talking.

You probably know Cutter's – it's the place down the road where the gnarled old landlord has been pulling pints for what seems like centuries and the usual gaggle of blokes hang out, few of whom ever seem to talk to each other.

There's the yuppie throwback who's still looking for Wetherspoons, the two builders propping up the bar, the bank clerk by the window, unemployed dad, and clean-cut genial guy, who looks for all the world as if he's the most popular guy in any gin joint in any town in the world.

What has the Bible got to say to blokes like them and me and you? The real question is, what hasn't it got to say?

I'm grateful that Dave Hopwood has asked me to join him for a pint along the road of life and faith, to make me think about some of the vivid, colourful stories that shed blood, tears and light across the Bible's pages.

Dave's a great bloke. I can vouch for him. So I hope you're willing to stop for a moment, to think, to listen, and to connect the Word to the world you're in. Life to faith, weak to strong, man to man.

Brian Draper, 2006

Introduction

If your life is anything like mine, you probably pick up your Bible and ferret about in it on very irregular occasions. Sometimes because you're in a good mood, sometimes because you're in a very bad one. Maybe because it fell open on the floor when it dropped out of a pile of magazines and you realise you haven't seen it for three weeks. Sometimes you throw it open because you desperately need to hear from your God and your eyes fall on that all-important verse from Proverbs 26:11: 'As a dog returns to its vomit . . .' Sometimes you're just curious.

I have to confess I've been spectacularly inconsistent when it comes to Bible-reading notes.

So when I was considering this book, the idea of wandering down to my local pub on a bad day and sitting there with a pint and the Good Book seemed like a good notion. The Bible is really all about life and this earth, not religion, so reading it in a lively, earthy environment seemed appropriate.

That's the reason that I've chosen a random selection of readings in no particular order. This is not a man who is diligently reading his way through Leviticus, as gripping as that might be. This is a guy who is haphazard and doing his best to make his way from one day to the next. So, he wanders down to Cutter's when he has a chance and flips open his black book anywhere and everywhere.

I've tried to pick passages that might appeal to a guy like me. That's really the only criteria for the selection you'll find here. I hope it makes you laugh, cry, get angry and get quiet. Perhaps all in the space of the time it takes to drink a pint.

Before too long you may notice that I have, ahem, 'played with the biblical text a little'. Some of the extra details have the authority of Scripture; some may be historically plausible; some are just from my fertile imagination! This is a deliberate ploy. In a poor attempt to bring the stories alive I have added tension and details, sometimes adjusting the order of events, and embellishing the characters. Forgive my Hollywoodised version – I hope it might inspire you to flip open your own dog-eared Good Book and see what really happened. (I've also taken some liberties when I've quoted the actual text. You'll see what I mean.)

If nothing else, I hope it helps you connect with the God of the Bible, who wired us up, will do everything he can to catch our attention, and allows us – no, wants us – to be blokes and have faith.

Dave Hopwood, 2006

1. Bathsheba's Bath

2 Samuel 11 and 12

The night is warm and dark; the man is distracted by thoughts of war. A million stars look down from above, like a myriad of stab wounds in a night sky jabbed to pieces.

The man stares ahead of him, through the open window, across the rooftops to the open country beyond. Territory thick with mantraps and mercenaries. Should he be out there with them? The other kings are away with their men. Plotting his downfall, preparing to split his dynasty and slaughter his men.

His men. Those hard-bitten dogs of war. Men who have followed him through thick and thin, through blood and bone, sweat and spit. They'd go anywhere for him. And now he's here, and they're out there. Dying so he can fatten his gut with good wine and rich food.

He loosens his belt, throws a glance at the stars and recalls the last kill of the last battle. Three Philistines caught with their pants down. Literally. Attempting to rape a farmer's wife. The God of heaven had made his sword swift that afternoon. He'd made no mistake there. Cruel men required cruel justice.

He had first spotted them splintering the front door with an axe and two spears. Right, keep going lads and you'll end up with more than a good time and sore groins. Flecks of white wood sprayed through the air like bits of skin as the men gouged their way inside. And then they stood gloating for a moment, wiping sweat and spit away before they drunkenly loosened their tunics and bore down on their prey.

He can feel the joints in his fist tighten as he remembers coming at them, like a beast from the apocalypse. Boy, how he hated bullies, men who took what wasn't theirs, and tore it up so it would never be anyone else's. He recalls the smash of his fist on the first man's face, blood spurting from split nostrils as the startled head cracked back and struck stone. He savours again the sound of the jabbing of his sword into the second man's gut, the twist and the cry of pain that followed, and at the same time the crunch as his sandal ground into the last guy's groin. You'll never do that again, big boy. Never. You should have stayed at home and left other men's wives in peace.

A sound outside his window brings him back to reality. Torches burn across the rooftops and he catches his first glimpse. She's there again. Uriah's wife. He can never recall her name but he won't forget her beauty. There are plenty of women in his life – but none like this one. He can't tear his eyes away. The robe slides over her smooth pale skin and she lights up the night like a goddess. She turns her head towards him; does she see him? He steps back into the shadows, ashamed of his secret interest in her.

He turns away and pours himself another goblet of wine. His head swims a little – perhaps he did well not to go to war with the others. He feels out of shape, he has no stomach for the fight tonight. Those three Philistines would have finished him on a day like this. He'd have been dead meat.

She reminds him of the farmer's wife. Vulnerable, young, innocent. He's been studying her for a good few minutes before he realises he's back at the window and wanting her again. Why do the women in his life not look like this? How can she be so perfect? She stands in the water and lets the soap glide off her. It's as if she's lonely too, offering herself, wanting his comfort, wanting his touch. Wanting to lie beside him in the king's bed. At least, that's what he tells himself.

He drains the cup and looks away, rubs his tired face with his tired hands. What's he to do? His body's on fire but he has no desire for the women he knows. He's too acquainted with them. He knows their every move. There's no excitement there, no romance, no mystery. OK, enough temptation now. He'll be strong, do the right thing. He'll finish up here, take a fresh cup of wine and go and write up his journal. Spew out his frustration across the page. He moves to the door. Pauses. Glances back. He's left his empty cup by the window. If she's still there it'll be a bonus. If she's gone, he'll know it was never meant to be.

They make love all night.

Even for him that's pretty good.

With each time the thrill fades a fraction and the stale emptiness creeps upon him a little more. Like slowly pulling a clammy blanket of regret over his damp body, a little higher, a little closer to his heart.

And each time her beauty fades a little too, and she looks more like the other women in his life.

He makes attempts to caress her cheek as she dresses and goes but he knows, they both know, sin isn't just crouching at the door. It's moved in, brought the family and taken up residence.

This is the start of something big.

Cutter's is the kind of place you go when the weather's grim and the inside of your head is grimmer. I often go there with my frustrations, my fears and a frazzled leather-bound book. The one with the edges stained and torn by some machine in a factory. A bloke's Bible.

Today is that kind of day.

I slip into the dimly lit room, order a pint of local ale and pull up an armchair. The fire's bright and spitting orange flame at me. That's the good thing about Cutter's, on the gloomy days there's always a fierce blaze in the grate.

The crumpled landlord behind the bar has been there for decades. He doesn't wear smart black waistcoats and serve up chicken wings with barbecue sauce.

He pours ale and he pours it well. His fingers are gnarled and grizzled from years of smoking woodbines and scratching at the engine under the bonnet of his ailing Jag.

He's not chatty and just nods when the need arises. He knows me and asks no questions about my dog-eared Bible. I wouldn't know what to say if he asked. I'm not that chatty either.

His daughter slips through the bar as I crumple in the chair and I'm reminded why I came. She's eighteen and dresses sparingly. I bury my nose in my pint and suck a third of it. Then I turn to my Bible. I know where I'm going – 2 Samuel 11 and 12.

David's in trouble – like most blokes I know. He's married and got other women on his mind. What is it they say about men and women? Blokes strike up like a match, women brew like a kettle. Well, she lit his torch all right.

So what's new? A cocky leader at the height of his powers comes crashing down. I think I've heard that one before. Power corrupts; absolute power – absolutely.

He has everything going for him – yet still he's insecure, still he needs to check if he can pull the birds. Still he needs to know he's got it. Maybe it was because he hadn't gone to war, like the other real men. Maybe he was just bored. Maybe he watched her night after night, like his favourite website, promising himself that each time would be the last.

That's the problem with sex, isn't it? They say it's like other addictions – but it's not. You have to buy alcohol, you have to brew coffee, you have to shop for chocolate and clothes. Your body parts are right there for you – open all hours, 24/7. Accessible day or night. Combine that with the pornographic world in your head and the shop's never shut.

Even as I sit here supping my pint I can think high and mighty one second, down and dirty the next. I can ache to heal the world one moment, undress a woman the next. What am I to do? What do I find in these disused pages that gives me hope?

The king plays the knave and has his way. Lucky him, he has everything, doesn't he? Money, sex, power, and now even more sex. He has it all . . . Or does he? Maybe he just has that washed up, wrung out, *I'm rubbish* feeling I always get from sensual sin.

Sure, he feels worried. Worried that the world will know what he's done. For a while he buries his guilt, then a note appears on a silver platter lying beside his green figs. You're gonna be a dad. Let the cover up begin.

Got to hide it, got to blow up enough smoke to confuse the enemy.

So get the husband back, get him drunk and in the mood and send him back to the missus to deal with the problem. What a relief. How good must David have felt when he saw Uriah swaggering back home to his wife, half-cut and ready for action.

And how bad did he feel the next morning when he found out Uriah had slept badly . . . not because of his wife.

I know the story. As I flip the pages I know what's coming. David admires Uriah, he's a good warrior, he's an upright man and an honest citizen. He may even have been a good mate. But if he won't bed his wife he's no use to the king. Bury him. Put him in battle where his bravery is sure to get him killed. Then David can comfort the beautiful widow. Maybe his loins even warmed to the thought of that. Men can be like that. Good men can be like that. Even men who spend their lives chasing God's heart.

The king of hearts can be the Jack of lads.

He knows we are dust . . . As I pull on the last third of my pint the phrase rolls into my head like a lost marble. Coolly I flip to the book of Psalms expecting my eyes to instantly alight on the line. But they don't. They uncover some phrases about kneecapping my enemies so I move on and rustle paper until I finally find what I'm looking for in Psalm 103. Maybe David even wrote this after he'd been named and shamed by Nathan the prophet.

'He does not punish us . . . he removes our sins from us . . . he knows how weak we are . . . he knows we are dust.' David may well have penned these words after the whole Uriah chapter.

In my opinion, he certainly penned Psalm 51. And God did create in him a clean heart . . . But his family was scarred for life. One of his sons later tried a similar trick on his half-sister. Bedding her violently and then hating himself and her for his corrupting lust.

Men can be so stupid. A night of passion. Five minutes of fire. Either way we sacrifice health and dignity on the altar of our loins. And then we're trapped –

locked in the glittering cage, where desire breeds frustration, frustration breeds misdemeanour, and misdemeanour gives birth to self-loathing and bitter contempt.

Of course the obvious thing here is – I'm not alone. If Godly Dave can trip over his regal loins, then no one's safe.

As I glance up and round this pub from the cosy confines of my comfy chair it's all too plain. We look like regular guys on the outside. The yuppie throwback who stumbled on this place while looking for Wetherspoons, the two builders propping up the bar, the bank clerk by the window, the unemployed dad skulking in the shadows, even the clean-cut genial guy attempting conversation with the stoical landlord. We look like blokes who know what's what, been round the block a few times, dabbled in girlie mags and secret sex when we were kids but matured out of that now.

Truth is, we never do grow up, do we? We'll always be teenagers in the trouser department. Always Jack the lad in king's clothing. Those matches still strike so quick and easy. I don't know much about kettles, but one glance'll light this firestick; one look can be enough. One sliver of stray skin is all it takes.

To a man we glance up when the landlord's daughter glides past again. We each do it in our own inimitable fashion, but we all cop a look and for a moment the conversations turn stupid as our minds wander.

Men think about sex every six seconds, you know.

This is just another six-second moment.

I glance over my shoulder, expecting a latter-day Nathan to catch me out and tell me about stealing other men's privileges. But he's nowhere to be seen. Maybe it's because I'm not a king, or maybe it has something to do with the writings of an old, gnarled saint called Paul.

As I stand and steel myself for a trip down the high street, braving the onslaught of a hundred provocative hoardings and a million men's magazine covers, his words rattle round the inside of my skull.

'. . . I don't do what I should, always do what I shouldn't . . . can't escape that. Who's there to rescue me? Thank goodness – someone's taken the rap, stepped in front of me and put his body in the line of fire. I may fall and fall again, but thanks be to the God of heaven. His Son has sorted it.' (See Rom. 7:14–25)

2. Ehud's a Hood

Judges 3:12–30

Ehud stops to check himself in the pool of the palace grounds. Not a single drop of sweat on his forehead. That's good. Don't want to go giving the game away before the kill.

He's already sent the servants back. They were useful for buttering up the old scumbag with a few coffers of gold. But they've served their purpose now. It gave time to case the joint, check for an escape route, form a plan. So it's: 'Thanks guys, make your own way home.'

He'd waited till they'd all gone, watched the last shadows fade into the sun, then he'd turned back and retraced his steps.

And now he stands inside the palace grounds.

'Got a message for the king.'

But it's for his ears only.

The bodyguard pauses, licks his lips, a bead of sweat plays around his left eyebrow.

The minder knows King Eglon. He's an evil scumbag. Any chance of gleaning useful secrets and he's onto it. The minder looks at the guy in front of him. This Ehud can handle himself – but there's no weapon on his hip, and his right hand looks a little shaky anyway.

'This way.'

The minder's voice rattles like shaking a bag of gravel. His head indicates the door into Eglon's private chamber and the two of them cross the threshold.

The king's voice is sour.

'What is it now?'

Eglon is a tub of lard. A greaseball who can barely blink without breaking into a sweat. He's lying across a sofa like a massive bundle of dirty washing. Two half-naked women are draped across his bulbous thighs. Their warm dark skin is shocking against Eglon's slimy white legs.

'What is it?'

Eglon's fat tongue snakes across his fat lips. Daubs of stale fruit smother his chin and neck.

The bag of gravel rumbles again: 'He's back, the man with the taxes. Says he has a secret message for you.'

Eglon spits at a silver bowl and misses. A ball of green phlegm sits on his priceless carpet. He holds a gleaming hand up and waves at the girls. They sigh heavily and saunter from the room, one of them tutting as they go.

Eglon turns his hand and wags a fat finger at Ehud.

'You! What is it then . . . this *secret* message?'

Ehud glances at the minder; it's a quick manoeuvre, and calculated too. Eglon spots it.

'Get out!' he waves the fat hand at the bodyguard.

The minder doesn't sigh or tut. He just leaves. He can't afford to be puerile like the whores, he values his life too much. Eglon may be bisexual but the minder's just not his type.

Ehud glances about furtively.

'It's a message from God, my Lord,' he says.

Eglon sneers. 'I thought *I* was God,' he says. 'Am I talking to myself then?'

'You must decide that, sir.'

Ehud does not move. No mistakes. Wait. Wait for the call, wait for the moment. Wait.

Eglon tosses a grape and misses it with his mouth. He curses, shifts his weight and belches.

'All right, come on, come on. Get it over with.'

He beckons to Ehud and begins to stand. He never makes it.

Ehud is over there in three strides. In two moves he's leaning over the king and with one stroke the fat man is dead. He barely has time to expel his last breath.

Eglon's last move is to glance down at the left-handed sword protruding from his belly. Ehud gives the two-edged blade a final twist then stands back quickly so as not to get splashed. Eglon's intestines burst from the numerous folds of flesh and a ton of red and grey flops noisily onto the floor. Eglon lifts his head but there's no colour there now. It's all over. He falls on his expensive carpet and gets a faceful of tripe. There's a foul smell about the place as three days of constipation eke out the back end of the king and fill the royal pants. Ehud smacks a hand over his face, locks the doors from the inside and leaves through the sewer vent.

The landlord's daughter is called Stacey. I discover this by listening in on someone else's conversation.

She's wearing a silver crucifix round her neck and one of the builders is chatting her up. He's not your typical brickie, not all stubble, gut and builders' cleavage. This guy's sleek and well-groomed, more James Bond than Johnny Vegas.

They talk about the crucifix; it's probably his way into discussing deeper issues, like whether she'll go clubbing with him tonight in Carnal's Pickup Joint. Inevitably they move onto religion and she quickly and categorically denies any link between herself and the little man pinned to the metal hanging around her neck.

'Oh no, I'm not religious – spiritual yeah – but not like – you know – krischun or anything.'

He's mightily relieved and things look good for a night of clubbing and some extra curricular stuff.

Strikes me Christians can be a strange bunch of people. Get 'em on their own and the ones I know can be the kindest, most helpful dudes in the world. Stick 'em in a room together and they become downright weird. 'But Christians are just normal people!' I can hear my long-suffering wife cry somewhere in the twisted corridors of my head. Yeah, right – till you get 'em in a group together and call it church.

I leave the bar, take my pint and glance around as I ease into my favourite chair by the fire. Just the one builder today. No sign of unemployed dad or the bank clerk, and clean-cut genial guy is on his own, silently rearranging beer mats and looking, it must be said, a little on the glum side. I pull out my roughly-hewn leather-back and find it falling open at a sumptuous moment of murder and revenge.

This is a fantastic passage. I read it through once. Twice. Three times, barely able to believe the wondrous story of suspense and intrigue, assassination and flab.

The people cry out for a saviour and the God of the universe gives them Ehud, the left-handed Benjamite. I glance up for a moment, straining to recall the meaning of the name Benjamin. I catch Stacey's eye and she throws me an enigmatic grin. That throws me off my stride but I'm quickly back. 'The son of my right hand' – that's what it means, which of course makes this a great play on words. Ehud – the left-handed son of my right hand. Bingo. That's the key to this tale of derring-do.

Ehud is a professional killer, skilled in making weapons and using them, and he, it seems, is the perfect saviour for the people. This guy really is the next James Bond.

Why? Well, cut to the king's palace. The evil king Eglon is ruling with an iron hand, abusing the people and gorging himself on the fat of the land. Eglon is from Moab, and the Moabites took control of Israel when the people fell away from their Maker.

So Ehud goes to visit him, bearing tax money to soften him up. While Eglon eagerly fawns over his ill-gotten gains, Ehud cases the joint and spots a sewer for a getaway route. Puts me in mind of a scene from *The Shawshank Redemption*. Ehud says 'Ciao', leaves with his servants, then separates from them, sends them home and returns alone. Now comes the clever bit. Ehud gains access to the king and assures him he has an important message for him. He appeals to the king's ample vanity. Like something out of *The Godfather*, Ehud leans over Eglon, says, 'I've got a message from God for you' and swiftly stabs him in the gut. He jabs him so hard that the sword disappears into the copious rolls of flesh and Eglon's internal organs spill out all over the floor. Ehud then locks the doors and makes his escape through the aforementioned sewer, leaving Eglon's servants to surmise that the king must be on the toilet having a prolonged session.

The moral of the story? Well, why choose Ehud? Because of two things – his strength, and his weakness. Ehud was a trained killer; no good sending a vicar or a social worker. You needed a man with a sword and Ehud had plenty. But, he was also left-handed, and as such would have been despised in that culture. Ehud the freak. Can't even insult you with his right hand. No – but he can dupe you with it. Ehud conceals his sword on his right thigh, and unexpectedly for Eglon, draws it with his left hand.

I recall very few of Paul's famous list of spiritual hobbies in 1 Corinthians 12. But I bet a nutter to a fruitcake that Ehud's killer gift is not listed among 'em. Yet it was clearly there for divine employment. Good ol' Ehud. Despised in the playground, deadly in the palace.

Can't help wondering though what on earth this bloody gladiator tale has to do with me, sitting here in twenty-first century Cutter's today.

Then I glance up at the crucifix around Stacey's neck. That'll be it then. We always confuse cleanliness and Godliness. Just 'cause something's covered in mess doesn't mean it ain't righteous.

Eleven men looked at a twelfth on a skull-shaped hill and wondered what on earth that piece of beaten meat nailed to two bits of wood had to do with the future of anything. Surely that wasn't spiritual. Blood and gore and nails and torn flesh. Can't be anything to do with the God of heaven. And yet – centuries on – Stacey wears a silver crucifix. It was spiritual all right. Dead spiritual. And so was butchering Eglon.

There's another tale in my little black book. A tale without any sex, thugs or rock'n'roll. Two women become friends because of the men in their life. The younger, Ruth, had a son. And the son had a son. And that boy became the finest king Israel's ever seen. A fighter, a poet, a singer, a tactician, a visionary, a true politician and a man after God's own heart. And aeons later his royal line came good again. This time a boy became king, not only of Israel, but the world entire.

My bet is that royal line was only possible because two faithful, law-abiding women came to a place called Bethlehem and settled there in a time of peace. A time of peace ushered in by the brutal killing of an evil king at the hand of a left-handed assassin.

One big jigsaw. A perfect fit.

I down my drink. Smile at Stacey and her crucifix and slip on out into the dying day.

3. Job's Got Boils

Job 1 and 2

The sun rises on another day, blinking intermittently through the straggling lines of bulging grapes. The owner rises too, sits up and stretches. He reaches for his first cup of coffee, brought to him at the ringing of a distant bell. He sits on the gleaming white verandah and enjoys the first dark taste of steaming caffeine as he watches the children running barefoot in the olive groves below. The day looks like another warm one, the skyline is blue and clear. Beneath him, in the many bedrooms of his sprawling home, his family stirs after another night of partying. The sons he is so proud of, the daughters he treasures and protects. The grandchildren, who make him laugh so heartily, continue to run amok in the fields, doing more damage than good, but he does not mind; he has many more fields, only a limited number of grandchildren. Their happiness and well-being mean more than a thousand acres of well-kept land. Their cheerful freedom is worth its weight in golden barley.

A servant appears in the yard below, and the two exchange a few words, the master bestowing the day's doings upon the faithful butler, more a friend than a serf. Half an hour wanders lazily by and the family assembles for breakfast alfresco, a starched white table laid with the produce of goodness and mercy. There is much laughter, yawning, fresh fruit and warm bread. The children wrestle with their parents and the parents wrestle with each other. Their words tussle and their jokes jostle for first place, but the meaning is amicable.

More servants pass by, dragging bulky oxen and pompous horses. A few clouds saunter past, pausing long enough to admire the landscape before wandering off in search of more turbulent scenes to rain upon. The family makes their many plans, which include another party soon. They chart their summer and plot the farming months ahead. The grapes are looking good this year, the crop will be an extravagant one. The owner sits back and for a moment, just a moment, considers what life might be like if he were poor and alone. But his moment of consideration is a short one. He ponders for no more than a second, and then the morbid moment is gone.

Life is good. The future holds out a full fist of promise. He affords himself a smile, and his eldest son returns it. The day is a happy one, the man is mightily blessed. He is at one with the world and at peace with his God.

His name is Job, and before the day is out, he will have lost everything.

Scorched land lies before him now. Corpses litter the ground like tossed garbage. Stunted, twisted bodies of people he loved and trusted, their faces contorted in the black grimaces that accompany tortured death. The sun is high and it beats on Job's broken back. Tears won't come. His heart is too empty, his mind too bitter.

Where is the good way now? Standing at the crossroads of his own life, where is the promise that so many held out to him? He did what he could. He gave to the poor, he spoke up when cruel injustice crossed his doorstep. When the homeless came by, when the down-trodden called out. He was there. Always. He walked humbly, kindly, justly, and people knew it. They nodded and smiled, stood and shook his hand. No one was afraid to knock on his door for a leg up or a hand-out. Was that his crime? Too much fame in this life, too much recognition for days well lived. Or was the contributing sin delivered by his children? They were no worse than anyone else's. You bring them up as best you can and still they go searching for something to damage themselves with.

He always tried to cover their tracks, always did his best to bring them to his Maker in humility.

'The Lord gives and the Lord takes away. . . In this world there is trouble. . .'

Perhaps there is no more sense to it than that. Nothing else can explain how he could start the day with everything and end it with nothing. Less than nothing – with a deficit of grief and disgust and pain and fury.

He stands and stares at the smouldering embers of his house, at the charred bones of his children, at the torn seeping remains of his servants. Vultures tear at the bodies and wild dogs hang back, inching closer for a mouthful of human flesh.

Job turns and vomits. He has no stomach for this. He throws up the bile inside him, the agony and sadness that has pooled so quickly inside his body.

Cutter's is busy today. So busy that my chair is taken.

That's not fair. I'm on a bad day; the lout sitting in it sups weak lager and strokes greasy hair. He doesn't belong near the warmth of the fire.

It's raining out and I'm soaked. I chose to walk in from my home half an hour away, hoping to expel my bad attitude. Instead it started with rain only five minutes into the journey. Now I'm standing here dripping with a wall of bodies between me and the anaesthetic of that fine ale.

It gives me time to check out the competition. Men always do that, you know – jockey for position. Even if they know no one and will never see them again, they have to satisfy something inside that says, 'I'm better than you. I'm stronger, cleverer, better looking, faster on the finger, quicker on the trigger.'

I'm not. I fail in all categories. Even out-of-work dad seems more confident today. I satisfy myself with the thought that my daughter's cuter than their kids. It may not be true but right now, no one can prove it, so it's good comfort.

It takes so long to get to the bar I need another shave by the time I rest my elbow on the oak. The landlord greets me with his usual warm scowl. A nod and a raised eyebrow, today he won't even grant me the luxury of remembering what I drink. I force a smile and point. He nods again and sets to pouring.

By the time I turn back to look for a seat, they've all been taken. That means only one thing. I'll have to fight my way through to the pool room. It's not that I have anything against pub sport, I'm just in the right mood for sulking in my armchair, and breaking out of that mindset is tough.

I fight through, get the stiffest-backed chair in the world and perch precariously close to the back end of a jabbing pool cue. Sooner or later I'm going to lose an eye here. I know it. It's just that kind of day.

Somehow I drag my leather-bound book from my back pocket without drawing too much attention to myself. This is not the place people normally study the Scriptures. But even I don't care, I'm too bloody-minded

to be embarrassed right now. Black Sabbath come thrub-
bing out of the juke box and I settle down to some nice
quiet biblical reflection.

Then I see the man-mountain across the room – blasting
holes in me with his storm-front gaze. He's wearing a T-
shirt that says *Been there, done that, bought this*. And I'm
not going to be the one to argue with him about that.
He's glaring at me from his seat across the pub. His
stomach resembles the Millennium Dome and his beard
would supply enough Santas for the whole of East
Anglia. But it's his eyes. They're black through and
through. If they're the window of his soul then somewhere deep down inside he has the hole of Calcutta. He
comes from the mother of all dark places. And he's staring at me. If he was hosting a pub quiz I guess question
one would be: 'What you lookin' at?' No idea why he
hates me – but he does. And hell hath no fury like a
local in an English pub who doesn't like your eye
colour.

I shift uneasily for a while, start to sweat a little, read
the same sentence four times. My stomach turns over.
Twice. Now it's a battle between my dignity and the cur-
rent arrangement of my facial features. Either way I lose
one of them.

No contest. Goodbye dignity. I'm up and out of that
chair before you can say ZZ Top.

It's just not my day. In my rush to escape with my life I
take the wrong door and end up in the beer garden outside, minus my pint. It's a pretty place; many a family
has frolicked in this former meadow, many a male has
bonded here. But not on a scrag-end of a day like this.
The plastic seats are pooled with green water and the
ground is a sludgy cowpat kind of colour. I pick my way

between the expanding puddles and collapse on a seat in an even bigger one.

This has really not been a good day. This isn't right. This place is supposed to console me. Instead it's a foreign land. No seat, no fire, no drink . . . just the murderous eyes of Giant Haystacks in there. I'm a stranger in a strange land. Everything I had here is gone. And there's nothing I can do. Large dollops of rain splash and smear across the wafer pages, but I don't care. Let my Bible get ruined. Let it be forever marked by the mess of this day.

I flip it open and it falls on Job 29. Poor old Job. The good guy with the bad boils. People say this is a book about suffering. Well if it is, it's a terrible one. Way too long, no one ever reads it. Forty-two chapters that could have been dealt with in ten. Two great ones at the start, four at the end, then another four in the middle would have been perfect – instead of the thirty-six long and rambling ones they put in. I guess it's true to life – your mates are full of hot air and do try and give you all the advice under the sun. And that's what Job's mates do here.

But this book provides no answers. We know the reason for the guy's misery anyway. Job's in casualty because the devil and God have had a strange kind of wager on him. God believes in Job, the devil doesn't. The devil claims it's cupboard love, and God, who's a sucker for anyone who loves him, is so confident the devil's wrong he lets the bad guy get away with murder. But that's not really why the bad guy wants to make Job suffer. He's not really just fed up because Job brings offerings and says prayers. Hunting through chapter 29 gives the real clue. Job's a man of integrity. He helps the poor, the widows, the orphans, the strangers, the blind, the lame . . . This guy's Father Teresa. No wonder the devil wants him out of action – he walks the talk.

And as I sit out here, my jeans sticking to my legs, the rain picking its woeful way down my vertebrae, my fingers fumbling at increasingly sodden pages, I glance back at the pub and find he's still there – the black-eyed giant. Gloating in the window, giving me the evil eye. But I don't care right now. Maybe God and the devil are discussing me. Maybe God reckons my religion can take it. Maybe my day is bad because God believes in me. It's strange logic and I'm no Job. Maybe today is just hard because in this world I'll have trouble. Either way it starts to matter more to me what I do with the trouble, as minor as it is compared to slaughtered children and scorched earth. I am scared of the big guy. I admit it. I am angry at the weather. And I'm thirsty for another pint.

But it's the loss of control I find hardest to cope with; many moons ago I verbally surrendered control to the God of heaven, but now he's taken me at my word it's a little uncomfortable.

The Lord gives and the Lord takes away.

So where's it all going to end?

I flip to the last couple of chapters. The maker of all things shows up and shows him . . . all things. What's going on there? Why doesn't he tell Job what's been happening? All about the wager and the reason for the bad times . . .

Seems there's something more at stake. Something about getting to know the Creator better. Something about opening your eyes and looking at the world to see the One who wired it up. Listening to the cellphone of creation to find out who's on the other end.

Seems to me it matters more to God that Job takes an interest in him, rather than just the things he's provided. They're just a means to an end. So how does it all finish?

Well, happily ever after. More kids, more money, a bigger house. So things are looking good for me getting another pint then. But that's not the point, is it?

Something inside says there's only one reliable end really; only one that make sense when countless orphans and numerous widows face life every day on a diet of wounds and tears and dread and a handful of gritty rice.

Somewhere out there, there has to be a heavenly Provider who'll cross oceans and tread fire to become a heavenly Parent.

I tuck the soggy black book inside my jeans and take the long way home.

4. The Man Who Would Be King

1 Samuel 24

David crouches low behind a rock. A stray arrow glances off the rock beside his shoulder, showering sharp splinters across his face. He shakes his head, spits out a few stony crumbs. He's surrounded, not for the first time this week. Saul's men are like stormtroopers. Bodies like brickhouses, fists like hammers, heads like lumps of sun-baked mud. They're out for blood and won't rest till they get it. He shifts his position and a spear glances off his shoulder, burning his flesh hot and taking a strip of skin with it. The cut's not deep but the blood quickly seeps to the surface. David checks his escape route. Ten yards to the next rock.

'Lord, let me live,' he mutters. 'I'm not up for dying today. Protect me from these dogs. Strike them down, though they swarm like bees and blaze like a fire. Let them do their best to kill me and let it not be enough. You can do it, God, you got me through yesterday, and the day before that. Make it so I can join in the songs of victory with the lads in the camp tonight. If I don't live who's going to tell them about today's glorious victory? Who's going to sing your praises round the fire tonight? I'm not gonna die, Lord, I refuse to die. I'm gonna live, and I'm going to tell of what you've done. I swear it. Let's go.'

He's up and zigzagging to the next rock. On his way he scoops up the spear that snagged his shoulder. He doesn't know how, but he makes it. Against the odds he's crouching behind the next rock clutching an enemy spear. He hears footsteps in the dirt. Someone's come with him. He stands, turns and instinctively jabs the spear. A crunch as the metal digs into ribcage. A startled broken-toothed expression as the soldier realises he's in his last seconds. The thug raises a dagger but David's at him, ripping the weapon from his fingers and slicing the sand-speckled throat. The flesh under his chin yawns wide, grins a blood red grin, and the soldier drops. David puts a foot on the dead meat, yanks the spear free and runs for the next rock with a dagger and a spear. Arrows fly past his shoulder. He ducks and dives, dancing more than running. Somehow, he's still alive. As he crouches again he mumbles words as if in a trance.

'The Lord is my strength and my song, he has become my victory. The Lord is my strength and my song, he has become my victory.'

He repeats it again. A mantra to keep him alive. He whispers it in hiding, then yells it as he runs for the next crevice of safety. This time a crater beneath a fallen tree. He turns and spies at the enemy from this bolt hole. Six soldiers are left on the manhunt. Kill them and you're free. At least till tomorrow's dawn.

A cave. Just to the right. It's hidden from view, if he can roll free and slip inside they may go past.

'Now or never, giant-killer,' David breathes, 'now or never. . .'

As Saul's men close in and surround the crater they steel themselves and raise razor-sharp swords. Now they've got him, now they'll hack him to shreds. Piece by piece. But they won't kill him in a rush. They'll show him the bits as they cut them off. Two dark eyes peer out at them. Eyes wide and gleaming. He's scared witless.

A yell from the leader and six fists punch at the face. There's a yelp, a scuffle and a wild pig staggers drunkenly from the lair.

One of the men swears, another hurls his sword and spikes the beast. There's a squeal and then a thud. A dead boar, but no wanted renegade. David's gone.

The soldiers wait. They sit, scratch, drink and wonder their fate. Saul's on his way, and they've failed again. They hope and pray he's not having a bad day. He's been known to slaughter his best men when the madness grips him.

They don't have to wait long. They see him coming with a few aids and bodyguards and are standing to attention long before he arrives and dismounts. The king towers above them. No one's as tall as this guy. His face is hard these days and severe, his good looks ravaged by too much wine and paranoia. He stares at them, knows what has happened before they say a word. His men are fools and cowards. If it weren't true they'd be standing there now with David's head dangling by the hair. He slaps one, spits on another, and comes close to kicking a third. He's a powerful man but there's something pathetic, something impotent about his petulant defiance. Like a man embarrassed in bed.

He kicks sand and turns away. There's a cave nearby. He trudges inside, tired of the chase, tired of the frustration and anger. Once out of sight he hitches his skirts and takes a dump on a rock. His head is miles away as he crouches. It's safe and dark in here, he's in no rush. He's had enough of real life and its demons.

Twenty minutes go by and eventually he stands, bellows for some grass, and cleans himself up. He saunters back out into the sunlight and leans against the cave mouth, rubbing a hand through his greying, sun-bleached hair. Then he hears a footfall behind him. He turns. There's a man with a dagger and a strip of cloth. The man's eyes are wide, his breathing's coming in quick bursts. He looks like a madman. There are beads of sweat around his eyes and flecks of spit at the corners of his mouth. The king rubs his eyes, but there's sand on his fingers and the grit blinds him for a moment. The man speaks and he knows instantly who it is.

'I used to play for you. I used to calm you down. I was like a son to you. Now you send your best men to butcher me. Can't we live in peace?'

Saul brushes away the sand and blinks until he can see David clearly.

'I could have killed you today. I could have at least crippled you. Sliced through your ankles and stopped you walking forever. Your best men would have been wheeling you round like a broken statue. Why do you keep chasing me like this? I'm on your side. I could have sliced your throat in there. I don't want to. You're my king. I respect you. I love you. Let's put this feuding behind us. God's given us this chance. Look! I didn't cut your throat, just your skirts. The God of heaven gave me the opportunity, and now he's given us the chance to forgive and forget. He sees everything – he doesn't want this. He loves justice and mercy. You should love it too. Hate will just destroy you. It'll eat you away from the inside out, like red ants in a healthy tree. It'll gut you till you fall down, hollow and dead. Let it go. Let God show you who to fear. Let him do the punishing. You're dedicating your life to getting revenge. Dedicate yourself to something greater. Something that'll last forever.'

He throws down the strip and drops the dagger.

'You can send a thousand savages – I'll still be stand-ing at the end of the day collecting their dripping heads in a sack. You don't have Goliath or any of his brothers. What do I need to fear?'

Saul's blinking at him, his eyes gummed up from the salt and the grit.

'Is that really you?' he says. 'Did God really put me in your hands like that?' A sour laugh. 'I guess I've been a fool. I've been blinded, and not by sand or the sun.' He coughs, clears a dry throat. 'Will you forgive me, son? Will you promise you'll show the same kind of leniency to my family that you've shown to me today?'

'You still don't get it, do you? You still think I'm out to kill you. I'm part of your kingdom. Why should I want to bring harm on the throne I'll inherit one day?'

'I think you're right. You will inherit . . . Promise me David, that when you're king, you won't punish my family to get back at me.'

David looks disappointed, but he nods anyway and says the right words. Saul scoops up the cloth, barks at his men and leaves the dagger for David.

David slumps to his knees, relief washing over him. He takes the dagger and scrawls in the sand:

They set a trap for me, these lions, these killers.
Their teeth like those of a wild animal, stained with
     blood and bared for the kill.
They were sure of my death, certain of my blood on
     their hands.
But they forgot about you.
They forgot you are mightier than their traps
Higher than the heavens.

Never forget this day. Never forget that God's love is as
broad as the horizon.

His power's always evident in the people and places
he has made.

I don't normally find myself in Cutter's at nine o'clock
on a Friday evening – that's usually the time when
adventurous married men like myself are busy batten-
ing hatches and adjusting cosy rugs around our knees.
But tonight I've had a slight border skirmish with the
pocket of resistance. Actually, there was little about it
that was slight. We ended up spitting blood at each other
about who was going to shut the wardrobe door, change
the loo roll and pick up that stray wet wipe that's been
on the lounge carpet all week. Life can be fraught with
tough decisions.

So I did the mature thing and threw a strop, then
walked out on her, unravelling the loo roll, booting the
wet wipe into moist tissue oblivion and shot-gunning
the wardrobe door as I went.

And now I find myself discovering that Friday night
in Cutter's is not Monday lunchtime. The place becomes
the Hammersmith Palais – or at least attempts to.
There's a makeshift stage right in the spot where unemployed dad normally hovers so uncertainly. Cables and
microphone stands make the place look like NASA and
while the line up may not exactly rival Live8 – it does
feature some local colour going under such names as,
Pelvic Floors, The Hatchet Men, Serious Groin Strain,
Swimming in Sewage and Napalm Nuns. I walk in to
find three teenagers on stage in pinstripe suits and weld-
ing visas attempting to make more noise than each other.
I think they're doing a heavy metal cover of 'The Sound
of Silence'. It's not easy to tell because they're playing
the right notes, just not necessarily in the right order.

Apparently they go by the name of Two Boys in a Mood, and aside from the fact that they clearly can't count, you can't fault 'em under the trades description. They sound like just that. They're snarling, aggressive and every so often the whole place shudders with a sound akin to a bedroom door slamming. If this is 'The Sound of Silence', I can't wait for Napalm Nuns. Apparently they do a thrash punk version of 'Annie's Song'. Glorious!

I was in such a bad mood I didn't intend to bring my black book – but God must have shoved it in my back pocket as he chased me from the building. I find myself slumping down to find a huge wedge of leather jamming into my backside.

I angrily flip the book open, skip all the hopeful bits and turn to a suitably angry psalm. Good old David, you can always rely on him when you want a rant and rave. I skip a few verses about the wonder of all created things and land on a nice paragraph about the joy of kneecapping your enemies: 'Bless the little birds, look after the newts and mice, oh and please would you gouge out the eyes and hack off the reproductive organs of those who want to do me similar damage.'

People think this stuff's about happy songs of praise. Yeah, right. In some ways this stuff's more aggressive than anything Serious Groin Strain can come up with. David was the original protest singer, the first punk rocker. Life stinks! This ain't good enough!

I used to adopt this strange spiritual persona when I hit my knees in prayer. My voice took on a repentant sinner tone, it dropped an octave and sounded as if I were about to break into plainsong. I frowned a lot and looked as if I was trying to remember who won the Eurovision song contest in 1963.

Lately I've backslidden. I've taken David's advice and pocketed his insights about God knowing I'm dust, knowing my expectations of myself are far higher than his, not punishing me as I deserve. I've had the nerve to think the notion of a compassionate God might just be true. From time to time now I even manage to pray prayers that don't involve getting my spiritual donkey jacket out and putting on my 'sorted Christian' face. I'm learning a new language – a biblical one. It's called downright saying it like it is.

Bellowing at God might not yet be a regular feature on *Songs of Praise*, but when I think about my two-year-old, and how much honest angst he hurls at me without the slightest fear of rejection, when I think about my own reaction to his tears and tantrums, how I just want him to be OK again, how I just want him to stop fighting, how I just want to hold him upside down by the legs and hear him squeal with delight – when I contemplate all that, I reckon the Big Man upstairs can easily hack my days of white rage and blue language, my nights of black moods and purple fury. A good mate of mine just makes a joke of me when I ring him up and pour out my latest frustration. If he can laugh at me and diffuse the tension, how much more can the Creator of all good one-liners?

As I sit here now, sipping good ale and pondering the bad things in my heart, I long for a cliff edge somewhere, the wind whipping at my clothes, threatening to tear me off the land and into oblivion, and good old patient God, standing out there on the wild sea, not batting an eyelid, just occasionally mumbling a gentle word of invitation to step off the edge and let out all that's really going on.

I have spent so much of my time fretting about upsetting God. So many hours stabbing myself in the back before God does it for me. Then one day I stumbled on the third chapter of Lamentations and found an escape

clause. It's written by Jeremiah whose entire life was a
bad hair day. One day he comes home and throws a
hissy fit.

> I am the one who has seen the afflictions that come from
> the rod of the Lord's anger. He has brought me into deep
> darkness, shutting out all light. He has turned against
> me. Day and night his hand is heavy upon me. He has
> made my skin and flesh grow old. He has broken my
> bones. He has attacked me and surrounded me with
> anguish and distress. He has buried me in a dark place,
> like a person long dead. He has walled me in, and I can-
> not escape. He has bound me in heavy chains. And
> though I cry and shout, he shuts out my prayers. He has
> blocked my path with a high stone wall. He has twisted
> the road before me with many detours. He hid like a
> bear or a lion, waiting to attack me. He dragged me off
> the path and tore me with his claws, leaving me helpless
> and desolate. He bent his bow and aimed it squarely at
> me. (Lam. 3:1–12, NLT)

Here's a guy who's seriously miffed. Like the epony-
mous Bruce in the movie Bruce Almighty he's basically
swinging round on God and yelling, 'You suck!'

I glance around at the locals in Cutter's. Unemployed
dad – how often has he wanted to do that? Maybe he
does do it. Maybe he's not even sure God's there and listening but he still does it.

I guess that's one of the great advantages of having
faith. You believe there's someone out there taking your
verbal. How come I've been so sure my wife and friends
are big enough to take my worst rubbish and yet when
it comes to the guy who set the earth spinning with a
quick flick, I somehow find it hard to believe he won't
smite me off the face of that very planet?

Yet it's here in black and white; not only did these guys spew out their bile, they left it here on the page so that generation after generation could read their rantings.

So back to David and his cave-dwelling days. In the passage he's with his men but in my mind's eye he's alone. Like all of us guys. Alone and trying to survive in a world where he's got to make his mark. He's hiding in what turns out to be a public toilet. He's scared right down to the lining of his stab-proof, lion-skin pants. Crouching in the darkness, excruciating cramp creeping up the backs of his legs, he mumbles a heartfelt, desperate plea.

> O Lord, how long will you forget me? Forever?
>   How long will you look the other way?
> How long must I struggle with anguish in my soul,
>   with sorrow in my heart every day?
>   How long will my enemy have the upper hand?
>
> Turn and answer me, O Lord my God!
>   Restore the light to my eyes, or I will die.
> Don't let my enemies gloat, saying, 'We have defeated him!'
>   Don't let them rejoice at my downfall.
>   (Ps. 13:1–4, NLT)

I read those words when I'm feeling fed up because I've got to baby-sit again when I really want to go out and watch the new Bond movie. For David they meant what they said on the tin. His enemy did have the upper hand. His enemy was winning, on the verge of using David's head for an ashtray. Not, 'God is in control,' no sign of 'He's got the whole world in his hands' – no, instead it's 'How long will you look the other way? How long . . .'

Then his royal Saulness slips in for some light relief and suddenly hope winks at David in the darkness. David's too loyal to bump him off, but it's enough to prove he could have done.

Suddenly there's a way out. A way back from the brink of death.

When I dare square up to the Truth, when I acknowledge what I'm really thinking and spew out the acid, suddenly there's room to manoeuvre, room for some hope. When the bleak outlook has been dumped on God, then maybe I can see a way through the coming storm. Somehow.

> But I trust in your unfailing love.
>   I will rejoice because you have rescued me.
>   I will sing to the Lord
> because he has been so good to me. (Ps. 13:5,6, NLT)

But not until the anger's vented. Not until the poison's been extracted from the wound.

Woe to me if I dare live with a thin layer of *nicing* covering the rumbling guts of my passion and fury. If the God of heaven can't take it, then I'd better not dump it on anyone else.

So I down the rest of my amber nectar. Leave the screeching likes of Serious Groin Strain. Pick up the black book and head out into the night. I trudge for a while, end up a million miles from anywhere, and find an unsuspecting brick wall. Then I pause, take a breath and yell at it for ten minutes. When I feel empty, I turn and walk away, wrung out, but ready to return, like an ageing prodigal.

As I go I notice an old man peering out of his curtainless bedroom window. The poor guy's not heard language like that in a long time. I glance up, and he's startled. Then he does an odd thing, he smiles, and I somehow know – it's not just his face throwing me that look. Somebody up there likes me.

5. Adam's Best Mate

Genesis 2 and 3

Adam looks up at the gaping pink mouth and ponders. He has this strange ache inside, one that this slithering hosepipe creature – he's contemplating calling it a snake – can't possibly satisfy. The lonely ache began, oh sometime back there, he can't quite place the origin; maybe he always felt it. He only noticed it when his friend left.

It's been busy today. A million creatures strutting, slithering, marching, stomping past. No time for food, he'd had a working lunch whilst naming the canines. His mate had come in on one or two decisions, but mostly it had been Adam's lot.

'Anything you want, call 'em anything you like, I'll go with your decision.'

So he'd made up names and caused his friend a lot of hilarity. What's so funny about dung beetle – that was the more acceptable version, anyway. Sugar gliders, that was another choice that amused, and duck-billed platypus.

One or two of his names had not made it past the censor. Stupid-looking fishface, his mate had not gone for that one. Nor gullible mug, stinking fathead, evil-looking pantshead colossalbottom, and of course Hannibal the cannibal. But the others had been OK. Elephant, panther, monkey, monkfish, raptor, skunk, piranha, unicorn, cockroach etc. etc.

Problem was, having named them all he wasn't sure he'd remember who was who next time he saw them. He was pretty sure he'd mix up the meerkats with the giraffes. As far as he can recall, the meerkats have got long legs and necks like periscopes. Whatever a periscope is.

But now the creatures have gone off in twos and he's left propping up the bar all on his own. His mate's disappeared and left him with this dull ache. Something's not right. He thought the purpose of the day was to sort this thing out. Settle it once and for all. And to cap it all, this creature shows up with the glinting fangs and the tiny yellow-black eyes. It's an emerald boa, or maybe a parrot snake. Yea, that's it, it's a parrot snake. Same colours as one of those birds that wouldn't shut up about pieces of eight and being a pretty boy. It's just sitting there, arrogantly hugging a tree and accusing him with the occasional flicking of its gruesome tongue.

'Well, buddy, you may look like a million dollars, but I'm the one in charge, and you can hiss and not blink at me all day, it won't alter the food chain. So get over it.'

The parrot snake stares on. That little slimy tongue flicks out again; there's a whisper of a hiss too.

Adam stands stretches and goes looking for someone to talk to. Not that there's a huge amount of choice. He finds his mate leaning on a stick.

'Hey, how about a drink?'

God looks up. 'Is it that time already? Sure.'

God shins up a nearby tree, plucks a green coconut and tosses it down to Adam. He throws it so hard it bowls Adam over as he catches it. God plucks another and shins back down. The two of them stroll down to the water, cracking jokes as they go about gullible mugs and stupid-looking fishfaces. The man breaks off a couple of reeds, they jab them through the tough skin of the coconuts and suck on the sweet nectar. It's perfect.

'I've been thinking . . .'

They both say it at the same time, and both shut up simultaneously.

'You first, Adam.'

'Well, today was a good day. I love the job, it's going well, lot of job satisfaction, had to work through lunch but apart from that, the hours are OK. It's just that . . . I dunno . . . these creatures, they're amazing, but . . . I can't relate to any of them. I feel . . . stuck out on my own. Isolated. Like I'm in a box. There were times when the place was seething with bodies – but it was almost as if I was the only guy in the garden. Like I was all on my own. Maybe I need to look harder, the apes looked kind of friendly . . . Bad mannered, but friendly. Terrible bodily functions of course.'

'Adam . . .'

God pauses. 'If I make another one like you, it might jeopardise our friendship. . . Plus, the more people in the world, the more complicated it gets, the more risk that something might go wrong.'

Adam nods. But it's clear to God now. He is lonely.

'Come on, let's go swimming. We'll come back to this tomorrow.'

Before Adam can argue, God picks him up and chucks him in the water. He dives in after him and they vie for supremacy, pushing each other under until they're both spent. They lie on their backs in the water and watch another big screen sunset.

'You know the first thing I did when I made the sea? I went swimming. All day. Snorkelling, diving, surfing. That's why it took so long to make everything you know. Light for example. When I made that I just spent all day on the switch going click-click-click-click – on-off, on-off – it was so cool, I'd never seen anything like it before.

Light-dark, light-dark. Don't ever move so fast Adam,
that you forget to mess about. One day you'll have kids
– and if you've forgotten, they'll remind you.'

'Kids?'

'Yeah, little people, chips off your block. They'll do
what I did when I first saw the world. Play, dance, sing,
wrestle, shout, laugh, cry, scream, draw, paint and run
like the wind. You know, when I finished the globe – I
ran. All over it. Fast, fast, fast, feet caught fire a couple of
times. I just wanted to explore, to see it all, the heat, the
cold, the ice, the fire, the winds, the jungles, the swamps,
the lakes and the mountains. I went everywhere.
Everywhere. Your kids'll do that.'

'Where will these kids come from?'

'Yeah, good question. I've decided what to do.
There'll be another you Adam. You won't be alone. She'll
be like you, just different.'

'She?'

'Yeah, she.'

God turns to swim away, then pauses and looks back.
'But Adam – one thing.'

'Yeah?'

'Don't you forget about me.'

Some nights I can sit in Cutter's surrounded by people
and feel as if I'm the only one there. I can sit there hog-
ging my private seat, clutching my beer and my Bible
and feel a million miles from everyone else. Unable to
cross the divide. Desperately seeking solace while desperately longing for love – though I'd never call it love.
A laugh, a joke, a listening ear. Someone who 'gets' me.
Someone who laughs at the unspoken jokes, hears the
hidden cries, spies the inner torture of my soul.

Apparently it's an epidemic. This loneliness thing. It's
worse than traffic accidents or sexually transmitted

diseases, though how you measure such a thing is anyone's guess. I suppose if I'm lonely, the chances are, so are you. And if you're lonely, so's he, and her, and them over there. The yuppie throwback who's still looking for Wetherspoons, the two builders propping up the bar, the bank clerk by the window, unemployed dad, even clean-cut genial guy who looks for all the world as if he's the most popular guy in any gin joint in any town in any world. And of course, old gnarled fingers himself, the crumpled landlord with a drink and a grunt for anyone willing to cross his doorstep.

How d'you define loneliness? It's similar to the one about how d'you define boredom? Being bored, being lonely. Doesn't say much, does it?

Maybe loneliness is the absence of someone who understands. In which case no self-respecting Christian should ever have a problem. God's your friend. Jesus is always with you. Sure. But as one guy once said, he doesn't play golf.

I'm desperate for something more than this. But to express that desperation would put me in another league. The league of wimps in Cutter's, the league of needy in Christendom.

So what am I to do? Thank you so much, Adam. You had it all. You had what every guy wants. Untroubled relationship with your missus, uncomplicated friendship with God.

Most blokes aren't that fussed about fruit anyway. Why did you have to show such an interest?

A familiar sound cranks out of the pool room. Bono agonises about climbing highest mountains. He still hasn't found what he's looking for and neither have I. I want what Adam had. I want that relationship with the God of heaven that doesn't feel like a relationship with the God of heaven. The one that feels comfortable, easy, a friendship with a good mate who understands. Who walks through fire for you. Who'll wrestle tigers and build bonfires with you. The guy who'll stand with you outside a roomful of hostile interviewing executives and remind you to imagine the high-flyers in there without their clothes on. The guy who gets your jokes and gives you new ones. The guy who makes you laugh at your fears and failures. Snaps you out of the black moods that vice-grip the inside of your skull like a face-hugging alien. You get the picture . . . I want the perfect soul mate.

And instead I have Eve.

Still, it's worse for her. She's just got me.

I fetch a second pint, nod at genial guy for the first time in my life. He nods back but doesn't look so genial. Something's on his mind. He glances away, a frown clouding his features. Something's up. Maybe this guy needs a soul mate.

I glance back at crumpled landlord. He's taking an inordinately long time to pour this pint. I want it to be here quickly so I don't have a choice – I want to be forced to pay him and whisk away my drink so I don't have to consider the opportunity of asking genial guy how he's doing. I notice he's flicking the ring on his wedding finger. Maybe something's up at home. Maybe it's just what he does when he's stressed. Maybe he just thinks I look troubled and he's wrestling with whether to ask me if I'm OK.

The pint arrives. I pay. I leave genial guy. I sit down. I'm safe. But now my mind's in crisis. Why can't I just ask the guy if he's OK? Why am I so scared of making contact?

I take a hefty suck at my pint. It doesn't taste so good right now. I flip to Genesis. The start of it all. Adam's standing beside his wife, copping out while his soul mate looks deep into the yellow-black eyes of a parrot snake. There's some chat about trees and death. The snake makes up a whole load of reptilian rubbish. Eve, who wasn't there when the instructions were handed out, tells the snake a secondhand version of events. She's pretty chatty, but then, that's women for you. When Jesus met a woman at a first-century well he had a long conversation about spirituality and relationships. Still the stuff of women's mags today. When he met the guys out fishing, he just offered them a job.

I glance back at the bar. Genial guy's staring into his empty pint glass. I could offer him a drink. But then maybe he'd think I was trying to pick him up or something. I look back at Adam. His best mate's walking in the garden. It's a cool evening. The place is perfect, or so it seems. God's looking for his friends. Maybe he wants another swim, or he's got an idea for a new shrub and wants to tell someone. Maybe he thinks 'evil-looking pantshead colossalbottom' wasn't such a bad name after all. Either way he can't find his friends. He wants to sit on a rock with them and watch another big screen sunset; this one's gonna be a good one. He should know. But where are they? He starts to shout, to yell, to bellow.

Eventually there's a whisper. He listens again. The crack of a twig and hurried voices in the bushes. And the sound he's never heard before – the sound of shame. He calls again and a flushed face protrudes from a bush. It's Adam. God glances at a nearby tree. There's a space where a piece of fruit should be.

'Adam . . .'

God glances back at the tree. He knows the world has fallen. The whole of creation has slipped on its axis, and it'll never be right again.

It amazes me that you can read this account as God has to go on a detective hunt to solve the mystery here!

What's extraordinary too is that God doesn't mention the full impact of the crime.

There's no placing Adam in quarantine until another Adam can turn up with the antidote. God doesn't push these miserable sinners away. Instead he sits on a rock with them, kills an animal for them (maybe it was the unicorn), and makes good quality clothes for them. He teaches them to sew. Talks to them for a while about sin and consequence, and then he goes away for a think – and maybe to sob his heart out and beat his head against a wall. And when he comes back he has worked out the first in a long line of attempted solutions to the problem. Adam and Eve can't live forever now. One day his friends will die.

I think about the whole darn thing. I think about the cover up, the hiding in the bushes, the animal sacrifice and the clothes. And I know. That's why the thought of extending a hand to genial guy brings me out in a cold sweat. I don't want to come out of the bushes. I'm too vulnerable. I need the skins of my pint and my comfy chair.

But I go against type. I stand. I reach for my wallet. I'll buy him a drink. I cross to the bar.

He's gone.

6. Born to Be Wild

Judges 13

A nameless woman sits huddled in a field, her knees pulled tight to her chest. She's lost in a trance. Wondering. Waiting. Hoping. She can't have children. She and her husband learnt the hard way, through agonising years and months, beginning hopefully when they were first married. 'Will it be this month? Well, maybe next month then.' On and on. Month after month, year after year. Each time hoping, waiting. Getting close to the end of the cycle. This time looking good. But no – it's just late again.

And the anger. Her husband punching walls and drinking too much. Losing interest in sex because it's too painful to get your hopes up. What was once exciting now carries too much baggage. Can't just make love, we're making babies now.

So he's given up. She hopes he's just out drinking with other men on those lonely late nights. Not sleeping with other women who don't want babies, just some money in a jar by the bed.

And now this . . . This strange glimmer of hope. A stranger appeared, making promises about a baby boy. She could barely take it in at the time. It's too sick a joke if it's not true.

She ran to her husband and told him. At first he laughed it off, a bitter laugh that no one else would share. But later, for the first time in many a long night she caught him kneeling in the dirt. Mumbling, hands clenched, sending his desperate prayers to the God of heaven. He prayed for a sign. He prayed the man would come back. But she's convinced that's too much. He's testing God and now there'll be no baby. God will be vexed. It'll be too much for her husband who'll finally up and leave for good. God will punish her by taking her husband away forever.

She's wrestling with this now, clutching her legs and rocking gently back and forth in the field when suddenly there's a noise like the pearly gates slamming and two feet land with a smack in the dirt before her. She looks up, startled. It's him. He's back. And he's not angry.

'Wait! Wait here,' she pleads. 'I'll get Manoah. I'll get my husband.'

The man nods, walks to a tree and leans on it.

Before long they're back. Manoah is not cautious. He's way too jaded for caution.

'Are you the man who appeared to my wife?'

A nod.

'So, we're really gonna have a son. What did you tell her before?'

'Same instructions – no grapes, raisins, wine or alcohol. And no food forbidden by the laws God gave you. Don't worry, Manoah – this is not a bad joke. You'd better get ready for fatherhood, mate. This boy's gonna be sparky.'

They talk more, burn an animal as a sacrifice, and then fire falls and they stare in wondrous horror as the man steps into the flames, smiles at them and shoots heavenward like a ballistic missile.

Later, when the euphoria has faded, she's troubled again. Manoah's convinced, but she's scared. If this man really was from God, they'll die. She's been brought up to believe no one can come so close to God and live.

Manoah shrugs it off.

'Be logical,' he says, 'don't be so emotional. Would God have sent this man twice, taken so much trouble, if he's now gonna bump us off? Think, woman! Think!'

And so Samson is born. (And he's only the first in a line of brothers.)

What the heavenly man doesn't tell Manoah and his wife is that this boy will be a walking tornado. Killing men by the thousand, lions with his bare hands, and in the end, the entire Philistine leadership in one foul scoop. He'll also be hopeless with women. Running from one girl to the next, barely stopping for breath. Easily manipulated by them. Always hungry for another. Wanting everything he sees. Women will be his downfall and he'll fall many times. Till in then end, it'll kill him.

And through it all, the philandering and the carnage, the immaturity and the anger, the Spirit of God will weave his will. Until Samson's chaos brings order to a nation dominated by evil.

There are times when I revel in the sheer fact that no one has the foggiest idea where I am. I can be on a quick car journey somewhere, suddenly take a detour and find myself pulled over on a country lane, hidden below a suitable camouflage of overhanging branches, away from everything and everyone. And for one delicious moment, no one in the world knows where I am. I could be a single man again, an outlaw, a long distance runner, a backpacking traveller. I'm Maximus Decimus Meridius. I'm William Wallis. I'm Indiana Jones. I'm TinTin. I'm an indestructible superhero. I have no responsibilities and no dependants. No job I have to climb out of bed for every morning looking like the living dead, and no fear that I might one day lose it and find myself helpless, broke and out of control. I can be young and hopeful again, my days lying open before me like an unwritten novel. Action and adventure loom large across the pages. I can be anyone, I can do anything. Or I can be no one, and do nothing.

It's harder to imagine this sitting in my leather-backed chair in Cutter's. Pirates and renegades don't tend to park their backsides in comfy fireside seats, where they can bravely read the Bible and watch the world go by. OK, so Blind Pew visited the Admiral Benbow on a dark and stormy sign-creaking night, but that was to deliver the death blow to an old sea captain, not to snuggle by the fire and warm the cockles of his heart in a small town pub with antique pipes jutting from the ceiling and stuffed otters nailed to the walls.

So for now I have to settle for reading about wild men, rather than being one. And in my book there's no one wilder than Samson. Spoilt brat, intellectually challenged, Terminator by divine appointment. If ever there was a lone assassin – this is your man.

Yet there's an oxymoron here. This natural born killer has the most spiritual of starts to life. The Bible dedicates a whole chapter to the comings and goings of an anonymous angel of the Lord trumpeting the imminent arrival of the long-awaited baby boy to momma and pappa Sam.

Now impossible babies born to barren parents is no new phenomena in Bibleville. It's always happening: John the Baptist, Samuel, and, of course, Jesus himself. All birthed in the most unlikely of circumstances. But Samson himself is a complete oxymoron. So much time is spent describing the divinely crafted nature of this boy. Yet when he finally arrives, what do we find? The

guy's a spiritual pigmy. He may have the body of a
Greek god, but he has the personality of a Greek salad.
He doesn't know what he wants, but he wants it right
now.

A gorgeous Philistine virgin. That'll do nicely thanks.
The clothes off the backs of thirty innocent men. I'll take
those. Torching a few Philistine vineyards, seems like a
good idea. A thousand Philistine warriors. I'll have
them.

Again and again this loose cannon fires off cata-
strophically, leaving a trail of blood and destruction in
his wake. He's the most random of killer prophets. Yet
time and again my little black book assures me that this
genocidal joker is under God's jurisdiction. When the
spirit comes on him he slaughters. It's not listed in
Corinthians but he has the spiritual gift of annihilation.

And even though Sam seems to follow his own deca-
dent road less travelled – it's still running alongside the
path trodden by the God of heaven. Centuries later,
when some bloke put quill to scroll and listed the giants
of faith from days gone for a bunch of Hebrews, the
delinquent Samson is right in there, alongside the other
two-tone heroes.

Samson's been recruited to free his people from the
Philistine stranglehold, and though there's many a
peace-loving Christian who'd question it, in his own
stubborn way, he achieves it. He sets a cat among the
pigeons, and the cat's a feral, blood-spitting, heat-crazed
puma – striking when you least expect it, wiping out the
bad guys at the slightest provocation.

He must have been screwed up. Chasing after loose
women and sulkily scorching other peoples' back gardens are sure signs that a man is sixpence short of a fruitcake. Perhaps a strange sense of destiny made him an
isolated child, which in turn made him a difficult

teenager. Perhaps his parents found that a gifted son can be uncontainable. Did he have friends? Did he fit in? Did he get invited to parties and prayer meetings? I doubt it. It's more likely the great and the good crossed oceans to avoid him. Certainly eye contact was something to be eschewed. The term 'religious nutter' was most likely invented for this guy. He bullies his parents, tricks his peers and purloins prostitutes.

Did he drive a wedge in his parents' marriage? Did the troubled child drive his parents further apart? Were they tempted to never, under any circumstances, have another one?

And now we've opened another can of worms. Here's one thing I've never understood: Those parents who, ailing under the weight of a difficult marriage, decide to have another baby to *bring them closer together*. How does that work then?

Before we had children, I had a best friend. Now, four years, two babies and 1,000 soiled nappies and sleepless nights later, I have a mother, a wife, and somewhere way down the list, the mortal remains of my best friend.

I think of the 5.30 wake-up call this morning. Seems weeks ago now. Just like the hundreds of 5.30 wake-up calls I've endured, every one of them carefully engineered to occur on my day off. Or my birthday. Or Christmas Day. Kids have perfect timing. The one day of the week when I get to sleep in, and I spend it headbutting the bathroom wall in time with the dawn chorus.

The bits of my wife's body that used to be mine have been hijacked by my kids. Romance, candlelit dinners? Slow sex on a Saturday morning? Huh, we laugh in the face of such feeble things. Who needs those when you can fill your time scraping Weetabix off the bath mat and vomit off the cat's back? Why on earth would we want to catch the latest must-see blockbuster in a plush, air-conditioned, sound-surrounded palace, when we've got 'Bob the Builder' on repeat play and 'Barbie Girl' pumping relentlessly in the background? Who needs sleep? Who needs peace and quiet and space to unwind? Real men live on the edge! Of madness. There are times, in the wee small hours, when our house resembles a bad day in Beirut. How come the product of love can threaten its very existence? Let's blame Adam. Or even better, Eve.

Samson's mum and dad must have felt the tremors; their world must have rocked nine months after the ground moved.

'Congratulations, Mrs Sam! You've got a healthy, bouncing baby boy. He's just outside at the moment, murdering sheep.'

I glance over at the bar. One of the builders is in with his girlfriend. She's flashing a rocky ring around, so strong possibility of marriage then.

I leap out of my seat. I tear them apart. I fling the ring, and yowl, 'Don't even think about it!' But only in the padded cell of my mind. On the outside, I'm as docile as a stuffed lamb. You see, like it or not – I believe in marriage. I wouldn't dream of sending these two lovers down another lane. I just wish I could make 'em see that the road before them leads to North Korea rather than Neverland.

We endow every wedding with fairytale glitter, don't we? Our own lives are such a struggle we need these little glimmers of gladness every so often. We need to pin our hopes on something. Maybe this time it really will be like the movies. Maybe Prince Charming and Snow White will stay forever on the page, and not turn out to be three-dimensional Victor Meldrew and Cruella DeVille. Apparently, most of the people who stay married do so 'cause they think marriage matters. It must be true, I heard it on the radio. The sweet and sour shades of romance disappear faster than a Chinese take-away. So you have to find something else to nourish the partnership.

I flip another page. And here's Samson, playing pick-'n'mix with his women. Commitment? What's that? A virgin here, a prostitute there, till he ends up with a hair-dresser who'll be the death of him. Short back and sides? That'll do nicely.

The love-struck builder's called Brian. I heard his name just now. He's staring deep into his fiancée's eyes. He wouldn't look so doe-eyed if his buddy was in. But he's not. Brian's alone; alone with the love of his life. The world around them has faded now to a distant fuzzy glow. They're the only two people on the planet. And the sky's about to fall on their heads.

I remember those magic moments. I often imagine them again when I'm alone in the car somewhere, hiding in a lay-by. For a split second I'm tempted to drag my wife from her bed and force her to glare deep into my bloodshot eyes, but I figure she's suffered enough. I'm with Robin Williams in *Good Will Hunting*, lamenting the loss of his wife and singing the virtues of marriage to young punk Matt Damon, telling him there are things about his wife only he knew.

It's true. And my wife 'gets me' in a way nobody else does. My sex life may be as interesting as my sock drawer, but I know things Samson never learned. I don't think he ever got close to sucking the marrow from life. He just nibbled all over the place and spat most of it back out again.

In many ways, Samson's a child of our time. A real twenty-first century boy. Russell Crowe, Wayne Rooney and Pete Docherty rolled into one. I could envy his frenzied freedom. His life of thrills on a stick. As long as

I don't mind the loneliness, the mood swings, the self-destructive tendencies and constant smouldering frustration.

This lonely loony certainly is a man for *his* time. For twenty years he's a slayer politician. Reigning when nobody else wants the job. Killing Philistines in a time when Philistines were to be feared, not fought. But Samson fears no one. And maybe that's his true strength. Almost in spite of himself he did what was ordained from the heavens. Sometimes courage and madness go hand in hand. Maybe that's why he's listed as a hero of faith. If nothing else he stood up against evil oppressors.

Brian and his girlfriend leave wrapped in each other's gaze. No doubt their bodies will soon follow suit. I'm left alone with my book and my beer. One's much easier to finish than the other.

No idea what became of Sam's poor mum and dad. Perhaps they lived out their years in relative peace and quiet. Perhaps they were murdered by vengeful Philistines as they slept in their beds.

We'll never know.

7. The Horror, the Horror

Psalm 31

Have mercy on me, Lord, for I am in distress.
>   My sight is blurred because of my tears.
>   My body and soul are withering away.
I am dying from grief;
>   my years are shortened by sadness.
Misery has drained my strength;
>   I am wasting away from within.
I am scorned by all my enemies
>   and despised by my neighbors –
>   even my friends are afraid to come near me.
When they see me on the street,
>   they turn the other way
I have been ignored as if I were dead,
>   as if I were a broken pot.
I have heard the many rumors about me,
>   and I am surrounded by terror.
My enemies conspire against me
>   plotting to take my life.
(Ps. 31:9–13, NLT)

In the Nowogrodek Ghetto in 1943, an extraordinary escape took place.[1] Polish Jews ravaged by years of beatings, starvation, humiliation and living in subhuman conditions, dug a corridor underground and slipped out under the noses of their German oppressors.

These were people who were living on next to nothing, sleeping six, eight, sometimes fifteen to one room. Most of them forbidden to leave the ghetto, they were subdued by systematic shootings and public punishments, and frequently subjected to the appalling spectacle of their neighbours, friends and family being rounded up and transported to 'work' in the east. This offer of work of course, was nothing more than a cover for the highly organised and heavily regulated gassing and burning of millions.

Many died from starvation, many froze to death from the harsh winters, some committed suicide, many were slaughtered. But a few, a remnant, escaped – including a group of 100 who spent eight months secretly digging a tunnel under the town. The workforce included carpenters who stole wood and electricians who designed and installed lighting along the passage. The architects carefully designed the route so that it was deep enough to pass under roads transporting heavy lorries. Practises were held to acclimatise the people to travelling underground, and the yellow sand from the tunnel was smuggled out in hand-sewn bags and hidden in lofts.

These were people who had been ignored as if dead, and surrounded by terror; misery had drained their strength; sadness shortened their years, their bodies and souls were withering away. Their enemies conspired against them, plotting to take their lives. Yet they lived. They defied the odds. They refused to give up and die. And not only them. Their escape was set against the backdrop of an uprising in the Warsaw Ghetto. Armed Jews lived in the sewers and took on the might of the German army – living scarecrows picking off battle-hardened, highly skilled, well-nourished troops. Several times they beat the army back and reinforcements were called for. Eventually the soldiers triumphed, the heroes died, the houses were burnt and the ghettos liquidated.

But the Nowogrodek invaders were astonished to discover a tunnel under a bed and 250 people missing. Sixty mistakenly wandered back into the town and were rounded up. But the remaining 190 slipped into the forest and joined the partisans.

As I sit here by the log fire, watching the orange and yellow flames spitting at each other and jostling for position, as I feel the warmth and hear the crackling of wood, my damp spirits come out of the gutter and take refuge in this smoky haven. I sigh, sit back and flip through my little black book with its frayed edges. And it reminds me. Again and again it reminds me that there are places out there, in the real world, where fire is not the stuff of cosy nooks and gentle pints. Fire is the stuff of petrol bombs, civil unrest, rioting and intimidation. It's the stuff of death – and very little glory.

I have to face the fact that tonight, right now, fire doesn't just warm hearts and thaw toes. It robs people of their homes, their health, their hope, their dignity. Instead of giving comfort it takes lives. And in the wrong hands – it's genocidal.

My little black book is full of this. Hard, cold, stale reality, served up in stark, less-than-glorious Technicolor. It doesn't hide it, it doesn't lie. People can be bad. Very bad. And often the good people do nothing.

'We must never let it happen again . . .' The seven best-meant but most useless words in the history of the world. We might mean them with every ounce of sweat in our skin, but most of us have more chance of riding a unicorn across Xanadu. Even as another cautionary reminder of the holocaust is released, so another genocide sparks up somewhere. Rwanda, Uganda, Iraq, Zimbabwe, South Africa, Bosnia, El Salvador, Indonesia, the Sudan, North Korea, Russia, China, Cambodia . . . They all have their grisly tales to tell.

I don't know what David was going through when he wrote his thirty-first psalm. I don't know what he feared. Probably Saul bearing down upon him again, with more stormtroopers than you can shake an olive branch at. They didn't wear jackboots, or carry cattle prods. But they might just as well have.

How often did Jesus glance at a distant murderer, hanging like so much raw meat on a cross, and flinch? How many times did he wake abruptly in the night, disturbed by dreams of what would come? He was surrounded by reminders of the brutality of life. Roman soldiers sneering and swearing. Badly built towers collapsing and crushing innocent people. The poor and the sick clawing at him for help.

'In this world you'll have trouble . . .' He knew that well enough. Then he said, 'Chin up, I've overcome the world.'

But he still let the world do its worst to him.

Cutter's is pretty full tonight. All the regulars and plenty more besides. The gnarled landlord never changes though. Packed or empty, he just takes his time. Same old speed, one pint after another. The odd whisky here, occasional white wine there. He fought in Korea; I wonder if he learnt patience living in a hovel underground with too many men and a bundle of rats. I once took a trip to South East Asia. Cambodia. Spent a wretched afternoon in a place no one's heard of. A former high school named Tuol Sleng which became S-21 – a chilling interrogation centre. It's a compound, four buildings, three floors, little cells and large classrooms.

As you walk around you're confronted with barbed wire, iron shackles and hastily constructed isolation units. Places reeking of torment, some with pictures to pass on the past. I stared at face after face after face. Fourteen thousand innocent people who suffered and died there. The place is a now a museum dedicated to these and the other two million who were starved, clubbed or worked to death by the murderous Khmer Rouge. Halfway round the tour I gave up. I needed air, I needed to look at something still living, even just a patch of scrappy grass. I needed to know that life had recovered, that people had found a way to carry on after all that. Real men don't cry. Well, I wasn't a real man that afternoon.

How many prayers go up? How many millions of strangled cries rise to the ears of the God in heaven? How many afternoons does he spend traipsing around the places of the dead? He once tapped a guy on the shoulder, told him enough was enough. Too much wickedness, too much torture and bullying. Time to call time. The guy built a boat and sailed into the sunset, just a few family and a lot of pets on board. Must have stunk like hell.

But all the bad people went. All washed away, no more brutality, no more pain. No more petrol bombs. For a week or so. Then it all came back. Bit by bit. Freedom of choice bred more freedom of choice, which in turn bred more freedom of choice. Until the world ended up like this. And now bad people can't be nuked from on high, because the Big Man made a promise. No more wholesale punishment. Now we have to wait for the dust to settle at the end of time.

David takes a few more minutes to scribble hope across the pages of his journal.

He turns his face to the skies and yells, 'Help! Get me out of here.'

Or perhaps, like so many others, he doesn't dare raise his voice, just lets the chaotic thoughts rattle around his troubled head.

'Help me Lord, help me. Get me out of this and I'll always believe in you . . .'

Either way, he gets distracted from the problem in hand and in spite of himself, starts singing the praises of his Maker. Before you know it he's going on about the great and the good Creator. And what's more he's telling other people to make sure they do the same. Fearful or not, for a while at least he remembers the God who wired him up.

The fire's burning down, the sparks look a little weary, a charred log splits and tumbles to one side.

The landlord's stopped pouring for a while. He's just stood by the upturned spirit dispensers, staring ahead. Does he ever think on these things? Did his career in Korea drive him closer to the God of heaven, or push him further away? Did he ever throw his face to the skies and yell for a way out? Hard to tell, as it's not an exact science. I know a man whose faith survived five years on the Burma-Siam death railway. Conditions so bad one prisoner died for every sleeper laid. He's a man of courage and faith and integrity. There's a Bishop who even found his faith in that punishing environment. Yet others came back from the wars to end all wars with their religion in a bin bag. Their faith had died with their many comrades.

I shut the little black book and utter a silent prayer.

'O LORD, I have come to you for protection; don't let me be put to shame . . .

So be strong and take courage, all you who put your hope in the Lord!' (Ps. 31:1,24, NLT)

---

[1] Based on an account in Lyn Smith's *Forgotten Voices of the Holocaust* (London: Ebury Press, 2005).

8. Peter Peters Out

John 21

When everything falls apart, when you fear the worst, when the night threatens to close in forever, what do you do?

You go back to what you know. You do the cosy thing, the familiar.

You go fishing.

At least you do if you're a fisherman.

The others aren't sure now. Is he Peter or Simon?

'You lot call me Simon now, right. The Peter thing's over. It ended that night. You know, when all the *stuff* happened. Come on, I'm going fishing.'

It feels good to push the boat out again, to feel the wood in his fingers, the wind tearing at his clothes, the smell of Galilee. This is where he belongs. This is what makes sense to him. What was he thinking of, trying to be some kind of do-gooding miracle man? He was never cut out for that. Simon shuts his eyes and feels himself begin to relax. The waves claw at the boat as they set out from the shore; the spray showers his face.

They gather the nets and toss them overboard. The men begin to chat quietly; they sound like they're relaxing too. Maybe things aren't so bad after all. They can take up where they left off. The business will pick up again.

Too long goes by without any action and it begins to
feel like déjà vu. Someone calls him Peter. Simon swears
beneath his breath.

'Give it some time!' he barks. 'The fish'll bite.'

They don't. They're conspiring against him; just when
he's beginning to escape the past it's all coming back at
him.

'Peter!'

He cusses again. Don't they get it?

'I told you, I'm Simon. Now what do you want?'

They shake their heads and one of them cusses back
at him.

'It wasn't us,' they say.

'Well, someone called me Peter!'

'Peter!'

It's not coming from the boat. Someone's yelling from
the shore. There's a distant figure standing there, wav-
ing, yelling. Simon narrows his eyes. What's going on?

For a moment, his blood runs cold. It almost looks like
Judas out there. But it can't be a dead man standing on
the beach. Strange things have happened lately, but it's
not a dead man there.

He rubs his eyes, strains to see again.

'Turn the boat around.'

They don't dare argue; Simon's a smouldering vol-
cano right now.

'Peter!'

Whoever it is, Simon's gonna sort them out about that
one.

'Get any fish?'

Some of the others shout back a no.

'Try the other side! I guarantee you'll get plenty.'

Simon's stomach lurches. He's been here before.
Another catchless night and another stranger trying to

teach him to suck eggs. Before he can stop them, the others throw the nets over the other side. Don't they know anything? Silence. Simon stands staring at the shore.

'Simon! Give us a hand! Quick, the net's tearing.'

John leans over.

'Er, Pete, I think it's him.'

If anyone else had said it he'd have smacked them. But he can't hit John. They've been through too much together. There's another shout from the shore.

'Peter!'

Something inside him snaps. He knows he's an idiot, but so what. He's over the side of the boat and running, like the Prodigal's old man, tearing through the waves. It's hard going but he barely notices and before long he's there, feet on the beach, face staring at Jesus.

'You didn't bring any fish,' Jesus says, a smile cracking his face. 'I only came for breakfast.' He thumps Simon's shoulders. 'Come on, make a fire.'

By the time they've done it, the others are there, hauling the massive catch up the beach. Simon takes control, yells a bit, and does some of the dragging. They gut some of the fish, cook them and eat. The others are laughing, swapping stories with the greatest storyteller in the world. Simon sits and watches.

Jesus dusts his hands and stands.

'Let's go for a walk.'

Simon's up front with Jesus. John's not far behind. The rest bring up the rear.

'It's good to see you, Peter.'

'But am I? Peter, I mean? You said I'm a rock, you were wrong. I screwed up big-time.'

'Simon.' He stops, turns, vice-grips Simon's shoulder. 'Do you love me? I mean more than this lot? Do you?'

Simon kicks the sand. 'Of course I do! But I can't do this. I can't be some do-gooder. I mess up. I'm too feeble, too angry . . .'

'Simon – shut up. I've got a job for you. I want you to look after this lot, and the others who'll come after them. You do love me, don't you, Simon?'

'Yes! But I don't know if it's enough. I don't know if I have it in me. I don't want to live that night again . . .'

'That night's gone, Simon. Look at them – they're like lost sheep. They need you, OK?'

They walk on, Simon glances back; John's within earshot of all this.

'Simon, are we friends?'

'Oh my . . . how many times do I have to say it?'

'Three times, Simon, that's how many.'

'Yes. You know already. You know what I'm like. You know I love you.'

'Good, then don't worry about the past or the future. You'll have courage when you need it. Believe me, Simon, you may doubt it now, but you'll be strong enough to die for me one day.'

Simon's stomach churns.

'What about him?' he blurts, jabbing an angry finger at John. 'Does he have to die, too?'

Jesus smiles. "None of your business, Simon. If I want him to live happily ever after, that's up to me. You think about you, and you think about me. Nothing else. Now, are you ready to be Peter again?'

Simon sighs. 'No,' he says, but there's a smile loitering round his mouth. 'But if you want it . . .'

'No! If you want it, Simon! You have to decide.'

They walk on. And Peter decides.

It's been a bad day at work. Too much pressure to compromise. Integrity? What's that? Humility? Honesty?

I don't think so.

'Take those things to your church, mate, but you won't need them here on the shop floor.'

So I limp through the day, feeling like an oily rag, then add insult to injury by taking home my disease and vomiting it over my wife and kids. For once she practically kicks me out of the house. She knows I'll come here, drink too much. That's history, not news. But she already has two little kids in the house, she doesn't need a third.

I drink half my pint by the time I've found a seat. Of course, true to form, the fire's warm and raging and the pub is suitably quiet – just a shame the only other drinker in the bar has pinched my seat. Slinking bar steward.

I slump in a window seat, feel my Bible punch into my backside and hurl it across the table. It falls open at a well-thumbed Gospel of John. Peter's having a bad day, looking glum and filled with self-pity.

I am so glad about the questions Jesus didn't ask. The promises he didn't extract. The kind of things you get pummelled by when you're a kid.

'Why did you do that?'

'Didn't you know it was wrong?'

'Promise me this will never happen again.'

'Are you sorry? Are you truly, truly sorry?'

'Don't ever do that again.'

None of it. He seems more concerned about the future than the past. It was the same with Moses. God shows up in a blazing bush and rather than ask a few delicate questions about a certain body in a certain unmarked grave back in Egypt, he's preoccupied with the future. Perhaps he's watched Moses toss and turn in the wee small hours. Perhaps he's seen every drink he swallowed to dull the pain. Perhaps, after all, the God of heaven really does 'get us' better than we 'get' ourselves.

Peter's been kicking himself while he's been down. Limping badly ever since those three little fire-lit sentences. What must have gone through his mind when Jesus suggested a fire? Another campfire. Not only a repeat of the first miracle – the miracle directly related to Peter's job – but a blooming campfire as well!

'Oh great! Just what I need to bring it all back! The smell of the smoke, the crack of white-hot wood. People standing around chatting and warming their hands. Thanks a lot.'

And with all that fresh in his mind, Jesus takes him for a walk.

'Let's sort it out, Pete, let's put it to rest.' But there's no time of prayer ministry. No sobbing repentance. No court of inquiry.

For goodness sake, doesn't Jesus understand repentance? Doesn't he know about confession and forgiveness?

It was the same lax approach when he threw a tortured glance at a thief dripping blood next to him.

'Remember me . . .'

The words are dry, muddled, barely cohesive . . .

'Are you sorry then, mate? Come on, you've got ten minutes before your body packs up. What about that list of crimes? And do you believe Jesus is who he says he is? I think I've got the sinners prayer tucked away somewhere . . .'

No. None of it. Nothing but simple, brutal grace.

'You'll be with me in paradise. You and me, today. It's a promise.'

The forgiveness of God is so unfair! So unbelievably unreasonable. We want punishment, we want retribution. We want protracted news stories and trial by public opinion. We don't want simple, swift injustice. We want you to get what you deserve. And in Peter's case, there's absolutely no reason to believe he won't deny Jesus again. There could well be a whole battery of cockerels lined up waiting to signal another cock-up.

Maybe Peter's actions speak way louder than any feeble words might. Perhaps his life's already radiating something along the lines of: 'I'M SORRY. I'M SORRY. I'M SORRY. I'M SORRY.'

We think words matter so much.

I'm on my third pint. Admittedly only three sips in. But the landlord perked up a little from his usual crumpled state when he saw me coming back after the second. I'm trying to appease something in me. Not sure whether it's the distaste in my soul after a disreputable day's work, or the fear of God at not speaking up to defend good practise, or just plain old family guilt at dumping all over everybody I once promised to love and cherish.

I throw a look towards the fireplace. The huddled figure is unemployed dad; he glances up at the same time, gives me an awkward smile. He looks as frazzled as I feel.

I always find it easy to do the stupid thing when I've got a few drinks in me. I don't know this man from Adam. I've constructed a bucketful of preconceptions about him, most of them preposterous and conflicting. I'm not even that sure that he's a dad. He just somehow fitted that mould.

For the first time ever, I'm sitting by my fire, in my pub, chatting to a bloke worse off than me.

He's not a dad, and he's not unemployed. He is called Adam though. And he does have lots of kids, just none his own. He's a teacher. And his life's pretty grim. He hates what he does and his girlfriend is pressurising him to start a family. I slouch, he sits, I listen, he talks. Only a fraction goes in of course. For Gromit's sake – I'm a bloke. The small-talk gene passed me by. But I nod and I frown and I even manage to laugh at one or two of his dodgy jokes. It strikes me it's my wife he should be chin-wagging to; she'd know just what to say. I'm just on an endless round of 'yes', 'no', 'right' and my best one – 'Wow!'

But he doesn't seem to care. At the end of it all he stands up, reaches for my hand (for a moment I panic that he's about to grab my pint), and pumps it enthusiastically. I don't know if it's the drink or if something really has improved, but I feel better.

That's the moment when I realise I've left my open Bible back by the window. Oh great. The two builders are sitting there flicking at it randomly.

'This yours, mate?' They say when I go over.

'Err . . .' instinctively, without even trying I put on a sort of, *oh I'm not really sure, it's something I barely look at* expression.

Is that the screech of tyres I can hear, or a cock crowing somewhere?

Eventually I give in and nod, not least 'cause they're looking at me as if I'm a loony.

I pocket my cherished black book and leave. Then I realise I'm still holding my pint so I have to creep back, slip it on the bar from a distance and run like mad.

It's too late, the landlord's watching my every move. He's even on the verge of grinning. I've really made his night.

9. No Bull Thomas

John 14:1–14

Thomas is already in a bad mood. Not too long ago he made noises about wanting to die with Jesus. That was before people really started talking seriously about killing him. Now it's a different matter. There's murder in the air and Tom's bricking it. Life's difficult enough as it is. Tom doesn't like being part of a crowd, and for three years he's had to live with this bunch of morons.

They nod like chickens at everything Jesus says in public then argue about it all in private.

Not only that but Simon, sorry, *Peter* and John get all the best seats and all the top jobs. What did they ever do?

And now here they all are, sitting around chomping down the Passover and the lot of them perching there grinning like monkeys. Why did he pick this lot? Why not people with a little more intelligence, guys with more integrity than a pile of donkey droppings? Why don't they question? Why don't they admit they don't get half of what Jesus is talking about? Why do they just sit and nod and pass another grape? If this is the truth it isn't setting 'em free. And now Jesus is waxing lyrical about his dad's house. Well, it must be heaven because Joseph's long dead and his place did not have many rooms.

'Don't be troubled. You trust God, now trust in me. There are many rooms in my Father's home, and I'm

going to prepare a place for you. If this wasn't the case,
I'd tell you plainly. When everything's ready, I'll come
and get you, so that you'll always be with me. And you
know where I'm going and how to get there.'

What!

What does he mean? Surely someone'll ask him?
Surely someone'll mention the simple fact that they
haven't got a clue what he's going on about? But no.
True to form, they're all nodding, oozing spiritual matu-
rity and benign wisdom.

'Sorry, Lord, I know this is going to sound like I
haven't just spent the last three years with you, and I
know I'll appear to be a complete doghead, but we have
absolutely no idea what you mean. So how are we going
to find the way? We have no map. No directions.
Nothing.' Thomas stands, he can feel the colour rising to
his face. 'And if this lot have more understanding than
me, then I'll eat what's on the bottom of Nathaniel's
feet.'

'Well, you may need to wash his feet at some point,
Tom, but eating it? No. Thomas, I'm the way. I'll show
you. I'll teach you, I won't flannel you, what I say is born
of truth. I'll give you what you need to find the place.
And you'll live there forever.'

At last someone else speaks up. It's Phil of course.

'Er, Lord, just show us God and we'll believe.'

Why does Thomas have the feeling Phil's wanted to
say this for the last three years?

Jesus rubs his tired face with his hands. The backs are
tanned and patterned with scars from his years of work.
He looks up; there are rings beneath his eyes.

'Philip, how long have I been with you? Have you not
cottoned on yet? Have you not sussed who I am? You
ask to see God, yet you've been looking at me all night.
You can't separate God and me. I'm in him and he is in

me. My words are coming out of his mouth. His words
are coming out of mine. If you can't believe because of
that, then at least . . . and it pains me to say it, believe
because of the miracles you've seen. But I'd rather you
just trust me, and look to me, not what I do.'

I went to church today. It's a rare occurrence for me at
the moment. Somehow sitting in rows, laughing at
cheesy jokes and singing lines like, 'Isn't he really rather
lovely' and 'Be all else but what thou art nought to me
save that thou be something else to me' seem a million
miles away from reality and the God who walks the brutal backstreets of my life.

I heard a sermon today. Apparently I need to get my
life cleaned up. If I do, fervent revival is sure to break
out and God will be happy. Never mind the evidence of
my black book which quite clearly demonstrates that no
one ever gets their life cleaned up. Even *Saint* Paul spoilt
this notion by admitting, in Romans 7, that he did all
those things he shouldn't do. Poor guy. He must have
been human. Samson was as much an oversexed, selfish
spoilt brat as you could not wish to meet, yet here's a
man anointed by the Spirit and heralded by angels, who
quite clearly furthered the kingdom of heaven on earth.

I had a traumatic experience today. I hugged some
people. Or rather, they hugged me. One of them made
serious attempts to kiss me. Had she been twenty and in
a crop top I might not have fought her off so avidly.
Sadly she was one hundred and twenty and I didn't
want to get her hopes up. Apparently this was 'sharing
the peace'. I felt like sharing a piece all right. A piece of
my mind. I have a hunch that half those people grin-
ningly embracing the other half secretly wanted to throt-
tle them. My brother-in-law says there are three kinds
of peace-sharers – huggers, kissers and shakers. I'm a

shaker. No doubt about it. Give me your hand, let me pump it sincerely, and then let's casually walk away. Let's face it, you wouldn't catch Peter kissing and hugging Judas.

So I escape. Just before the last hymn I slip out and slink off to that other place of worship. I run like the wind, fleeing my responsibilities and my conscience. My wife's left stranded, attempting to silence the two children she spends the rest of her time encouraging to communicate. Perhaps that's where the troubles begin; we teach our kids that God's house is not a place for laughing out loud or speaking out of turn.

I'm off to that haven of noise and bustle.

Cutter's is awash with kids. Can you believe it? Apparently Sunday lunch sees the place mimicking McDonalds. Single mums and bored dads spoon-feed their little darlings with chicken nuggets and exorbitantly priced lemonade. My comfy chair doesn't even feature. Highchairs and booster seats are the order of the day.

Unemployed dad-cum-child-unfriendly teacher is here with his girlfriend. They don't need a highchair or booster seats of course, they're just sitting there surrounded by a sea of them, both looking glum. He's glum because there are too many kids, she's glum because there are not enough.

He sees me as I hurry in and because we're blokes, and I'm not so drunk, and he's not so depressed, we act as if we never had that conversation the other day, never spilled our guts and told the truth. A single nod and we avert our gaze. Reality will have to wait until we're both in worse moods.

In the pool room, Led Zeppelin's crooning about heaven and that old stairway while Meatloaf look-alikes smack snooker balls and beer guts together. Should I return to the safety of church for tea in green cups? It takes me all of two seconds to decide. I'm off to the pool room.

My good mate's there again, the black-eyed, dome-stomached one who wants to tear me limb from limb and use my leg as a pool cue. This time his T-shirt says: *667: the neighbour of the beast*. Friendly. He's ignoring me now though. Not bothered at all about my offensive existence.

Feeling like a goldfish out of a bowl I attempt to look invisible as I lunge for the nearest chair. Of course, I'm not the only thing looking distressed – there's my frayed-edged Bible. I open it at the back and make for the nearest Gospel.

I once heard a monk say that we can all trace our spiritual roots back to Jesus. Jesus converted the twelve, the twelve converted the 3,000 and the 3,000 converted . . . er some people at a Saint Paul Gig during his World Tour. And so on. So if you go back and back and back eventually your spiritual time-travelling will lead you to one of the disciples. It's the only way you could have got your faith. Well, there ain't no doubt my family tree would lead straight back to Thomas. The few occasions he's given air-time in the Gospels it's always to make a daft comment and a refreshing change.

Jesus appears to the faithful after the resurrection. Who's missing when they take the register? Thomas. He was probably out somewhere being difficult. Arguing with some Pharisees when he was supposed to be buying some grub. The others sent him out because they were too scared to leave the building.

When our hero gets back with a bag full of BLT sarnies and a crate of Budweisers, they're all over him like a rash.

'We've seen him and you haven't!'

'You missed him, mate!'

Maybe Thomas is hacked off because they're all so cocky; maybe he's just tired of feeling the odd one out.

'Are you sure it was him? I know what you lot are like. You got "sucker" written all over your foreheads. Well I won't settle for anyone just showing up and claiming to be the one. I want evidence. I want proof. I want holes in his hands and a scar in his side.'

You see, Thomas won't settle for bull. He won't nod and smile and say, 'Yes, everything happens for a reason, all things work together for good, just let go and let God and it'll be all right on the night.' You'll have to explain the word *'platitude'* to him when you meet him in heaven. You'll be able to spot him, he'll be the one organising the alternative worship.

Thank God for Thomas, eh? Literally. Here's a guy who won't pretend. A guy who won't just toe the line because it's the thing to do. I wonder if Philip felt able to ask an honest question at the Last Supper because Thomas had paved the way for him?

Jesus says, 'You know the way.' The apostles go, 'Yes, we do.' Thomas says, 'No, we don't.' The apostles mumble, 'Oh – no we don't.' And bingo! All honesty breaks loose.

'I do believe, Lord,' says Philip. 'I really do – I'm just not very good at it. If I could, you know, see God . . . if I could just get a glimpse and know that you're really the One . . . if I could see that he's really up there . . .'

There are times when I look to the ceiling and, like Philip, just wish for a quick glimpse of the Boss. Something just to prove that all this stuff I hang on to is really real and not just my imagination. I know I'm not supposed to think like this – but these questions just slosh around my brain and seep out sometimes.

I guess Philip hadn't been mountain climbing that day when Jesus suddenly revealed 'the real him'. Peter,

James and John are just hanging about, waiting for
another parable when suddenly it's as if someone
switched the floodlights on. All this gleaming brilliance
floods out of Jesus, as if he's shed his human skin, and
they're left staring at him like rabbits caught in a full
beam. Then Moses and Elijah, who, if you hadn't
noticed, had been dead for centuries, show up in the
same outfits. Talk about defying the aging process,
there's no sign of decomposition whatsoever. No wonder the disciples wanted to build houses and stay up
there – for all they knew this was the high point of Jesus'
life. Why bother going back down to normality. This is
obviously far more spiritual than a load of old lepers
begging for bread. God won't want them to rub shoulders with the poor and the lame and the unbelieving
after this close encounter. But it's the opposite. No time
to hang around, lads, Jesus is all set to get *more* involved
with dull reality, not less.

Thomas wasn't with them up there in the smoke but I
wonder what he might have said if he had been.

'Lord, can we all get Day-Glo outfits like that?' Or,
"Moses, just turn this twig into a glow-worm', 'Elijah,
just call down some white hot fire and nuke the other
disciples, would you?'

(Moses, of course, got the chance of a lifetime that day.
Up till then he'd only seen the Promised Land from a
distance. First from Egypt, then from heaven. But here
he is, standing smack in the middle of it. Result!)

Maybe Thomas was supposed to be there that day, but
he got the hump and decided four was a crowd. And
that's one thing he never followed. A crowd.

The sea of infant bodies is beginning to ebb away.
There's just the debris of soggy chicken nuggets and
spilt lemonade. The screams have died down and the

landlord's come out of hiding. Before now, it was Stacey serving up the happy meals and fizzy drinks.

I guess my time's running out. The Sex Pistols come on the juke box hailing 'Anarchy in the UK' and there certainly will be in our house if I'm not back soon.

I down my pint and slip back through the other bar. Stacey throws me a sweet smile and for a second my spirits soar, till I realise child-repellent teacher and half the other blokes in the pub are also watching her every move. She smiles at them too.

Where did we ever get the notion that following God means following the crowd? Most of the time they'll just lead you up a blind alley. I avert my eyes and make for the door.

It's rumoured Thomas ended up taking the gospel to the sub-continent of India. If that's true, he went further than any of the other first followers. Not bad for a doubter.

10. Castration and Crucifixion

Acts 8

It's the heat of the day. The sun's beating down and there's a shimmering curtain between Philip and the horizon. He's hot, thirsty, he's been walking for a few hours. His tongue sticks to the roof of his mouth and his head swims a little. His feet feel like bags of wet salt and his body's shutting down rapidly.

Why did he trust his instinct? What on earth was he thinking about, taking instructions from a stranger? So what if the guy was built like a Terminator and had eyes like lasers, he's probably sat on a rock right now supping wine and having a laugh in the cool shade.

He raises a sand-blasted fist and shields his eyes. Is that a carriage? A couple of soldiers? Maybe it's another Terminator come to give him a ride home. Not that he has a home. Saul sent his temple storm troopers round to kick them all out and ransack their houses. He saw kids torn from their mothers, grandparents chained together, teenagers beaten across the face with sticks. He still feels sick when he remembers the screams and the noise of wood cracking bone.

He recalls another face; this one was bludgeoned too, his eyes blackened and his cheeks sagging open in bloody gashes.

'If people hate me – they're bound to hate you. But don't be deceived, persecution is a sign that you're on the right road. It's not a sign of God's curse. Remember Job, punished because he loved justice, mercy and kindness. Singled out because he broke the jaws of Godless oppressors and made them release their victims. The whole world will hate you because of your allegiance to me . . .'

Philip was one of the lucky ones. He got out before the soldiers came. He clambered out of a back window and staggered through the blackness like a madman, his clothes half-gathered around him, looking for all the world like he'd escaped from some asylum. Somehow he made his way to Samaria, desperation spurring him on. He slept in a cemetery, ate pigswill and dreamt about prodigals. Thank God he had no children. Thank God there was no wife.

And the next morning he balled up his courage, washed in a nearby well and did the only thing he could. He went to the synagogue and started preaching. If he was gonna die, he might as well go down fighting.

He'd not been at it long when the unthinkable occurred and an old priest pitches up with a dodgy foot.

'I've heard about your Jesus. Well, he fed half a million people, they say. Can he straighten my ankle?'

Philip's in no shape for performing miracles. On the run for his life, ritually unclean, scared to death.

'He loves you. He died for you.'

'My foot. Can he fix it?'

A crowd is starting to form. There's nothing like embarrassment for entertainment value. Philip glances around at the faces, most of them sneering.

'Give me your foot.'

'Oh, I can't lift it.'

'Shut up and give it to me.'

Philip kneels, mumbles the kind of thing he's heard Jesus say a thousand times and then stands up.

'Off you go, then.'

'What?'

'Try walking.'

And the rest is history. The old guy goes running and leaping and almost gives himself a hernia. Thankfully he doesn't as Philip's not sure he's got the faith for that one. But others come. There's more prayer, more power, more people.

That was three days ago, and now look at him alone in the desert. He was almost a superstar in Samaria, people bringing him the best food, offers of free accommodation; he even signed the odd autograph or two. So what's he doing here, sweltering in the sand, shedding sweat like water from a leaky fish tank.

A carriage pulls up across the road. It's the business. All gold and silk and overdressed servants. An Ethiopian appears at the window. A servant opens the door and a regal figure steps down. He's carrying a scroll. The lackeys ply him with water and grapes. Philip licks his lips, and somewhere in the back of his head a voice whispers, tells him to get off his backside and ask for a drink. He doesn't need telling twice.

'What are you reading?'

The stranger looks him full in the face. The man looks powerful, but not proud. He stands straight as he holds out the scroll.

It's the prophet Isaiah, prophetic words of sorrow. Philip nods.

'You know this?' the man asks.

Philip nods again, tries to look casual. His eyes flick to the jewel-encrusted water flask.

The Ethiopian glances at the sun and rubs the back of his neck with a white-gloved hand.

'It's too hot for walking out here. Can we give you a lift?'

Before he knows it, Philip's jammed in the carriage, pouring sweet water down his throat and starting to feel alive again.

'I don't understand this,' the man's saying. 'Is he writing about himself? Is this man a eunuch?'

Philip chokes on the bottle and falls forward spluttering.

'What?'

'Is he a eunuch? Look, he writes like one. "He was humiliated, led like a sheep to the slaughter, and he won't see his descendants".' The man leans towards Philip. 'You see,' and his eyes glance down at his lap, 'I know about eunuchs.'

Philip wipes his mouth with his hand and offers the flask back. There's water all over the carriage floor, but he hopes the Ethiopian's not noticed.

'This is what it's like,' the man goes on, jabbing his finger at the scroll, 'this is castration. The degradation, the torture, the lonely nights of bitter regret. What does God know of that? Is the prophet a eunuch?'

Philip shakes his head. 'I never met him, but I doubt it. You see . . . He's not talking about castration – it's crucifixion. The man he means gave up everything, his life not just his loins. But he does know about degradation, torture and regret. I should know, I was there, cowering in the shadows. Have you seen Roman efficiency? Well you'll know what I mean then. This man, the man he's writing about there, is innocent, no – more than that, he was one on his own. Unique. Perfect. Nothing wrong in him. Nothing. Look, flick back to Psalm 22, see that? "My God, my God! Why have you forsaken me?" That's what he yelled as he was dying. Have you heard the sound of nail hammering through bone? God punished him instead of punishing the rest of us. One man – that man – volunteering for the rest of us. God so wanted to get to know us that he took the life of his only son as a scapegoat. Those verses there, that's what it was like. Everyone mocked him, enemies surrounded him like a herd of fierce bulls. Soldiers ripped into him like roaring lions attacking their prey, they swore and spat and shook their heads, saying, "Is this the one who says he's from God? Well, look at him now." They couldn't see it, they just couldn't see it. Those thugs murdered him.' Philip's face turns bleak for a second, then a smile cracks across his lips. 'But he wouldn't stay dead. They knocked him down, but he got up again. Three days in hell and he was back. Smashed open his own grave with his bare hands. And now an angel tells me to stand by this road and wait for you. D'you think there might be a message in there for you somewhere?'

It's a warm evening. A few couples are sitting out the back. It's unusual for this time of year. And more to the point – there's no fire. My armchair is sulking there, hunched in the cold light of evening, looking smaller and shabbier for some reason . . . Like a little scolded dog. There are no cracking twigs in the grate, no tongues of fire or glowing hearth. Beer gardens may be perfect for a family of five, but I come here to escape that. I come here to inhale wood-smoke and gaze longingly into the ever-changing flames.

I buy my pint and sit grimly by the cold grey grate.

I take solace in one of my favourite daring tales. Philip turns into Captain Kirk, beaming down in the middle of nowhere and then taking off again as soon as he's done.

I used to think that my little black book was full of saints and heroes and superstars. People who lived and operated in a different kind of world to mine. A place where people heard God all the time, booming in a Pythonesque fashion out of the sky. Divine lights zapping people and villains becoming heroes overnight. The land of the Old Testament was littered with the scales that had fallen from people's eyes, a land of discarded contact lenses.

Now I know different. Now I see that God, in his journey through time, has chosen to work mostly through the downright down-to-earth. After all, reality was his first creation. Why wouldn't he celebrate it and make good use of it? It explains why Jesus was often cautioning people to keep schtum about the dramatic healings they received. Nowadays we produce movies and programmes and entire TV channels centred around dramatic healings and signs. Back then it's as if miracles were more of a contractual obligation. Part of the story, but not making the front page. Not something to shout about. It sets me wondering whether miracles are the fast food of religion. Satisfying for a short time but really only creating a hunger for more of the same. Certainly if you follow the Israelites out of Egypt and across the desert it appears that a diet of the supernatural does not create a hunger for God. And so the God of heaven becomes more covert, more shy. An undercover deity working through the normal and the subtle.

And this is what we find here. There's no flash of lightning, no megaphone in the clouds. Instead there's a man reading the Bible and a bit of it leaps out, very likely because of his own experience. Eunuchs have been led like a lamb to the slaughter, they've been humiliated, they won't see their descendants. Whichever God is behind this Holy Book – he understands the lot of a castrated man.

Same today really. I open my black book, read a bit then look to the skies, with a kind of perplexed *how the heck d'you know I was thinking that*? look on my face. This also explains why often, when some verse leaps out, slaps you round the face with an orange glove, and jabs you in both eyes, when you try and find it in a different version it doesn't seem to quite work. God seems to select a bit for that time, in that moment, from that version of the Bible. It's not really transferable.

Of course – I'm not saying I'm not into miracles, or that I don't want them. I'll have the extra large carton please. The Jurassic family sized tub, thanks. But if I really want to grow up a bit and get to know God better I have a hunch I need to open my eyes in the mundane and the random, in the bad and the boring. I have to check out the concrete and the clay, the grass and the grit. In the warm evenings and the cold fires. In the happenings of the day, and the still of the night.

As someone once said, 'Coincidence is God's way of remaining anonymous.'

11. The Glittering Cage

Proverbs 5 and 7

He's tired, he's stressed, and he's argued with the girl he loves. So he left, slamming the door as he went, and now he's alone. Staring at a beautiful woman. She's standing in a street doorway, licking her lips and looking out at him. She blinks occasionally, her eyes are perfect and invite him in.

Soft music plays somewhere in the background. There's a bottle of wine in the fridge and candles in the bedroom. Her body is young and soft and just what he's looking for. He can smell her perfume . . . she smells great, and her smile is overpowering. He's been here before, many times. Standing on the outside looking in. She offers him so much and it costs him so little. Why doesn't his other woman understand? Why isn't she like this? Why doesn't she take so much time to get ready for him?

He knows her name. It's right there in front of him. Whether it's her real name doesn't matter. He likes it anyway. He stares at her again, tormenting himself. She licks her lips again. He licks his.

In his mind he's already inside. Undressing her. Getting her to do the things he likes. The whole thing is intoxicating.

He hears a noise behind him and turns away.

She's standing behind him looking hurt. She's caught him out again.

He looks at her, hangs his head and turns back to the girl in the doorway.

He reaches out a hand and shuts down the site.

The fake girl disappears and he's left alone with the real one.

As wise old King Solomon says in Proverbs 5:3–5: 'The lips of an immoral woman are as sweet as honey, and her mouth is smoother than oil. But the result is as bitter as poison, sharp as a double-edged sword. Her feet go down to death; her steps lead straight to the grave.' (NLT).

It's been a strange day. I lost control of it early and never got the wheel back. And it started so well too. My wife and I woke early and took advantage of a rare window of opportunity to buy a ticket for that great fun-ride of marital rumpy pumpy. Only to find that 'the time of the month' had kicked in early. Oh great. That left me frustrated and dealing with the problem in the shower, which in turn left me angry at myself and fearful of God for the rest of the day.

I take my seat and instantly sense it's still warm. Hello . . . Who's been drinking in my chair? Then I spot the magazine. Not just any magazine. But one of *those* magazines. OK, so it's not in-yer-face *Playboy* or *Men Only* – but it's still got a pair of boobs big enough to float a battleship on the front, with the offer of plenty more inside. Thank goodness I've grown out of all that. Thank goodness I've moved on. Thank goodness I no longer get a rush of blood to my loins when I see female flesh. Thank goodness I've . . . Oh, who am I trying to kid?

Of course I still get that same injection of mixed feelings. Excitement initially, the old schoolboy urges flood back, the 'I can't believe my luck that someone should leave this within harm's reach.' This is immediately blended with the reaction 'Oh heck, who's watching and will they think I bought this incriminating thing?' It's not mine, it's not mine, honest. I just came here with my pint. It wasn't me officer. Chuck in the final ingredient of, 'Uh-oh, better not waste time meditating on this, it's the fast lane to nowhere' and you've got a potent cocktail.

It begins with the eye-boggling glimpses on page three and ends with . . . Oh all right, it never ends . . .

Let's be honest. Many men – in fact, all the men I know – married or single, masturbate. And a lot of them look at forbidden fruit on their way to doing it. We hate it, we hate ourselves. Yet we keep coming back to the tree.

There's nothing quite like flying solo for offering you one hell of a rush and leaving you with just the hell bit. Completely wrung out. You start off wanting to get down and dirty – and that's just what you end up feeling – down and dirty. Roll up, roll up. Get your highest high and your lowest low all in the space of time it takes to log on.

These days, of course, looking at porn is perfectly acceptable. It makes for the best jokes in the best sitcoms. And you don't have to come right out of the closet and buy *Big Girls for Big Boys* or one of those other incriminating periodicals totally dedicated to DIY. Nowadays it's quite acceptable to buy one of the mature alternatives: A better class of soft sex monthly which also features tasteful articles on music, films, fashion and the best websites. Walk into any newsagent today and you can pick up your monthly copy of *Girl on a Stick*,

Schwing, Quickie, Eyeful and *Oggle*, without any need for embarrassment or a brown bag. There are even daily newspapers dedicated to it.

I've often wondered why it's mostly women who do the campaigning about the proliferation of sexual content on offer these days. I guess it's because the blokes, with the best will in the world, often feel compromised by it. On a good day we may be out there protesting with the best of them, on a bad night we could be in a darkened room, downloading the next quick fix.

So what's to be done? My little black book affords precious little space to commenting on the number one male hobby. One thing does seem clear. Hero after hero messed up on the sex front. Time after time after time. Samson wanted every woman he saw. And yet here was a guy spiritually marked from birth. Solomon, ahem, the wisest man who ever lived, had 700 concubines. I doubt if you have much need of a copy of *Women Weekly* when you've got live porn at the ring of a bell. Even good old Paul, after berating the Romans for six chapters about their crimes and misdemeanours then came clean and admitted he was in agony because he couldn't do the right thing. He knew well enough what he should do, welcome to the club Paul, but he couldn't resist choosing the other alternative. (Mind you, I'm not saying his sin was definitely sexual. Surely not you, Paul!)

I guess the blindingly obvious thing here is that these wayward dudes made it into sacred small print. They're all here, in my book of holy doings. Every one of them used by God in spite of their sexual shenanigans. The worst part of masturbation is the after-burn. The guilt, the self-hatred, the morbid fear of punishment and being thrown on the spiritual dunghill. How can you expect to be useful, or even worse, spiritual, after just doing *that*?

How can the God of heaven even give you the time of day when your mind's about as clean as a used bog-brush?

I guess I can only look to back to Paul – all he could do was say a heartfelt 'Thank goodness' for Jesus. Paul's life might have been smeared with sleaze but because one man's body absorbed the fallout from sin, then there was still room in it for God to use him big-time. But if I risk going the other way and just say 'Hey – it doesn't matter', well, where does that end?

As I sit here minding my pint and letting my eyes wander lazily over the full frontal cover before me, it strikes me the problem comes at me on several fronts. Does it make me useless to God? Straight answer has to be no. My black book is chock-full of guys being useful on a bad day. Honest answer is – it sure *feels* like it makes me useless. Does it hurt me? Any high's addictive, isn't it? Sugar, ciggies, sausages. I guess I was designed not to make it through the day without my fix of God, so you could say it's a design fault. I have a vacuum in my life for something more. My continuing problem is I want to cram it with the kind of stuff that will soothe my lonely longings. Does it hurt my relationships with other people? Of course, all the experts will tell me it changes the way I see women and turns the high street into a cattle market. It also places impossible demands on the one I love. And I wouldn't want those pressures heaped on me. I mean, clearly I'm Brad Pitt, Rudolph Valentino and Clarke Gable in bed, but sooner or later even that becomes dreary. (Surely not!)

Oh well, thanks, Adam. Thanks for eating that fruit and giving Eve the excuse to open up the first clothes store. Just think how much time we wouldn't waste if you'd have stayed innocent and naked. No long days spent in trawling round shoe shops and cardigan outlets. No need for all those gaudy catalogues taking up the space I need for my vital DVDs and CDs.

The word on the street is that you don't need to feel bad about masturbation. Just carry on.

The word in the church is that you don't need to feel bad about masturbation. Just stop.

I sigh and take a long final suck on my pint.

It's like an episode of *Taggart* with the last ten minutes missing. The tape cut out at the final advert break. Where's the solution?

Perhaps the solution is, there is no solution. There's just the grace to live with the tension.

12. How to Be a Shiny, Happy Person

Proverbs 3

My son, don't ever forget the things I have taught you. Store my commands in your heart, lock them away and melt down the key, for they will give you a long and satisfying life. Never let loyalty and kindness get away from you! Wear them like a 24 carat gold chain; write them deep within your heart, let them pump through the whole of your being. Let them influence every part of your life. Then you will find favor with both God and people, and you will gain a good reputation. Trust in the LORD with all your heart; do not depend on your own understanding. Don't despise your ideas and your passions. Treasure them and honor God with them. Seek his will in all you do, and he will direct your paths. Try the doors, keep moving forward. You can't steer an articulated lorry while the driver's sat in the lay-by chewing sandwiches. Don't be impressed with your own wisdom. God is always bigger than your ideas about him. Instead, fear the Lord and turn your back on evil. Then you will gain renewed health and vitality. And when evil ambushes you, when it overwhelms you and threatens to ransack your soul, tell him about it. Don't run from God in times of sin, run to him. He's the one with the anti-venom for that poison.

Honor the LORD with your wealth and with the best part of everything your land produces. Remember, your money is the address of your mind and heart. It will show you where your desires live. Then he will fill your barns with grain, and your vats will overflow with the finest wine. If they don't, don't panic. God will not necessarily make you rich, but neither do riches make you godly. My child, don't ignore it when the LORD disciplines you, when he stops you in your tracks, shakes you up and makes you think bigger. Don't be discouraged when he corrects you, when he gives you a good talking to. For the LORD works on those he loves, just as a father corrects a child in whom he delights. He'll tell you off one minute, then wrestle you to the ground and bear-hug you the next. He understands you are dust, he knows what you are like, he is realistic. He's not an ogre. He accepts you as you are, but he will not leave you as he finds you, he cares way too much for that. (Based on vv.1–12, NLT)

I bought a book today. One of those *Little Book of Witty Sayings to Make You Forever Calm and Happy*-type books. A book to help me be a better person. Had to then queue up for thirty-six minutes in the shop listening to the Cheeky Girls singing about their bottoms. Inevitably felt like jamming the purchase down the throat of the infuriatingly happy assistant.

So now I'm sitting in Cutter's with a pint of Guinness (and it's nowhere near St Patrick's Day!) and two books – the old lag being little and black and scuffed, the new boy little and calm and shiny.

My new book's called *Top Five Reasons not to Buy this Little Book: C.S. Lewis didn't write it, T.S. Eliot didn't contribute, Adrian Plass isn't mentioned, Billy Graham didn't edit it and Sir Cliff didn't write the foreword.* (A catchy title)

These names of course are machine-gunned across the front cover in bold raised lettering, and are the biggest thing about this little book.

Inside each page carries a top five list under a given title.

E.g.

- Top five sermon topics you hear all the time: Repent!, Convert Lots of People, Are You Absolutely Sure You're Saved?, Give Lots More Money, The Prodigal Son
- Top five, no six! sermon topics you *never* hear: Sex, Hell, Work, Life is Boring, Children, Reality
- Top five good reasons for not going to church: the sermon, the songs, hugging people, the coffee, the dance group
- Top five problems you can admit to having: struggling (in general), sinning (in general), feeling tired (in general), not understanding the book of Revelation (careful though, admit this in the wrong setting and you're in for a darn good pre-millennial hiding), occasionally missing your quiet time
- Top five problems you can't admit to having: lust, sinning (in any specific ways), boredom in church, planning to murder people, always missing your quiet time
- Top five, no four! books you can't read: *Lady Chatterley's Lover*, anything with 'Harry Potter' in the title, *The Da Vinci Code*, whatever is currently shaking Christendom to it's core
- Top five books you must read: the Bible, anything by Nicky Gumbel, anything with the words 'The Purpose Driven' in the title, whatever shook Christendom to its core twenty years ago, this one
- Top five ways to be really happy: pray a lot, let go and let God, smile all the time – even in your sleep, have a long and regular quiet time, dance in the Spirit

- Top five things you should wear: a beard, socks with sandals, a nice knitted casual vicar jumper, anything from the previous decade, anything with a fish on it
- Top five, no six! ways to stay sane: deliberately miss church every so often and go and do something you really enjoy, laugh at unintentionally funny moments in church, ask questions during the sermon, only sing every third word in a worship song and see if it makes more sense, sit in someone else's pew, avoid lists like this.

I pick up my other book of wisdom. The one jammed with sex and violence.

Strikes me there are a few key sayings missing from Solomon's little book of calm. For example, where's the famous *A bird in the hand is worth two in the bush*? Or *A moment on the lips, a lifetime on the hips*? And what about *As one door closes another one shuts*? *Buy one get one free*? *Don't pull that face or the wind might change* and *If I said you had a beautiful body would you hold it against me*? Where are all these gems?

Instead you get the world-famous Solomon and some bloke called Agur, saying things like: 'There are three things, no four things, that are never satisfied . . .' And, 'There are three things, no four, that amaze me . . .' Followed by 'There are three things that make the earth tremble – no, four'! Were these guys really that wise?

The book of Proverbs is a mixed bag, or perhaps a pick'n'mix bag, not unlike those you buy in a last minute hurry on a trip to the cinema to see the latest Bond movie. You run in, can't decide on a five quid bag of Revels or a ten quid tub of popcorn, so instead throw the nearest pink and blue and purple things into a bag and then spend the rest of the movie desperately trying to find something in there you actually like. Or is that just a matter of taste? Chapter 31 is famous for its description of the ideal wife. Industrious, tidy, clean, witty, rich and never has a headache. Very inspirational . . . Unless you are a less-than-ideal wife in which case it might really annoy you.

Chapter 5 is a cautionary tale and one for all us bozos who can't recognise an ideal wife even when she rises at four in the morning, buys a field and smacks us on the nose with it. It only applies to the simple minded who lack common sense – so . . . all men then. It's all about one of those top five items that rarely puts in a guest appearance in church.

But, as I flip through my leather-bound Bible, it's chapter three that catches my eye. This is the Sistine Chapel of the book, the DB5, *The Shawshank Redemption*, the 'Bohemian Rhapsody', the Kate Moss . . . you get the picture.

This is the heartbeat of true civilisation. Mercy, kindness, justice, humility and loyalty. The oil in the engine of God. This is not to be confused with the chip fat of televised civilisation. A globby cocktail of fear, cynicism, materialism, fame and – *reality* TV. An oxymoron if ever there was one.

The problem is, God's cocktail has such a bad press while the other one is advertised in pretty colours wherever you go. Singer Jack Johnson asked where all the good people had gone, and then proceeded to ask about the carnage he found on his TV. A harvest borne of selfish seed . . . Now there's a prophet if ever there was one.

But, it's easy to become critical and carpet-bomb the whole of modern life. What about Geldof with his insistent Band Aid that you just can't peel off and discard? Or the Make Poverty History people, or Amnesty International or a million other relief organisations? Of course the world is a bad place, but it's a good one too. And often where evil prospers, so does grace.

I can only look in the mirror and start there. I have an overpowering tendency to half-learn a lesson and immediately want to inflict the whole of it on others. Yet time and again, my little black book demonstrates that it's not what you say that matters, it's what you do. If I want other people to be more caring, just, merciful and humble, then I'd better start with me. If I make a fraction of a change in my life towards the good – then the world's a better place. Shame it's so hard to make that fraction of a change. I'd rather put it in a book and tell others to do it.

Living it doesn't make me so famous and important.

At least, not on earth.

13. Red, Red Wine

Genesis 9

It's a great day. The world just began again. A million wicked people had been water-blasted from the planet, God has high hopes. He beckons to Noah, leads him out of the ark and sits him down on a large rock. A rock not unlike the one he sat on when he made clothes for Adam and Eve.

On that day God made the first sacrifice in the history of the universe. Took an animal he loved and killed it to cover Adam and Eve's misdemeanour. Now he's made a bigger sacrifice. Slaughtered people he loves to salvage life from the wreckage that has become planet Earth.

He harks back to those early days and imparts the same kind of wisdom.

'Adam, Eve, Look! I have given you the plants throughout the earth and all the fruit trees for your food. And I have given all the grasses and other green plants to the animals and birds for their food.'

'OK, Noah, here we go again, multiply and fill the earth. All the wild animals, large and small, and all the birds and fish will be afraid of you. I have placed them in your power. I have given them to you for food, just as I have given you grain and vegetables.'

'Adam, Eve, I want you to multiply and fill the earth and subdue it . . .'

'Noah, have lots of children and repopulate the earth. Don't hang around, and stop that grinning. Just get on and multiply and fill the earth! Start competing with the rabbits . . .'

It's a fresh start!

Noah reinvents himself. He changes careers, leaves behind the boat building and takes up farming. He and his sons plant a vineyard. The soil's good, the climate's perfect. Before long the vines are sagging under the burden of Noah's first crop.

'Ham, I'm going out picking, you coming?'

'Sure, I'll be right there, Dad.'

'Shem, you wanna give your old man a hand?'

'No.'

'D'you want time to reconsider?'

'No.'

'Just give me a straight answer, are you coming?'

'No!'

'Don't mess about.'

'I'm not. I'm going fishing.'

So Noah heads out and starts picking. The vineyard is awash with the plump purple fruit. The day is warm and before long the sweat is trickling down Noah's face and running into his eyes. His hands are stained, his clothes spattered with juice. Ham appears and starts picking on the other side of the field. He's younger and faster, filling three baskets in the time it takes Noah to fill one.

'Dad, you wanna break? I got some water.'

Noah dumps his basket and trudges wearily towards Ham. Only it's not Ham, it's Shem.

'What are you doing here?'

He grins sheepishly. 'I changed my mind.'

'So where's your brother?'

Shem shrugs. 'Sleeping?'

They down the liquid and finish up. The whole ark episode took it out of Noah. He's looking older without looking all that wiser.

'Let's call it a day, Dad.'

The old man nods. Shem rescues the baskets and slings them on his shoulders. They head in and Noah takes a nap. Shem starts in on the grapes, tramping them and extracting the juice.

Every day they go out and collect more. Every day Ham promises, every day he fails to show up. This is a two fold operation now, picking in the day, brewing by night. Before long there's a barrel of something resembling wine. By now everyone's out there gathering. Parents, children, grandchildren. In the quiet of the evening, when the grandchildren are asleep and their mothers are minding them, he slips out of his tent and gathers himself together in front of the barrel. He takes a cup, fills it to the brim and drinks. The nectar tastes good. Full bodied, sweet, and . . .

He drinks some more. The world around him softens. He huddles up to the barrel and steadies himself against it. Just one more cup. Three helpings later and someone's shaking the planet. The ground won't stay still beneath him and it's hilarious. He tries to stand unaided and finds himself pitching forwards, he lands on all fours, jarring both wrists. But strangely there's no pain. He crawls on his hands and knees towards his tent. Which tent is his tent? He can't recall and they all look alike now. Mustn't accidentally crawl into the wrong one and scare the grandchildren. Or his daughters-in-law. As pretty as they are. His sons have pretty wives. Very pretty wives. As pretty as . . . Oh. His head feels bad. The campsite's spinning now and the tents are in a kaleidoscope. He shuts his eyes and puts his head on the warm earth. The ground is soft and comforting. Things begin to steady a little. He lifts his head, earth sticking to the right side of his body. All is well. The world is still now. And there's his tent. He stands up, puts his foot in a bucket of cold stew and falls headlong inside.

Five seconds later, he's asleep.

Ten minutes goes by and Ham returns to the camp. He's been out with his brothers, searching for new food. He wanders over to his father's tent and gets the shock of his life.

His dad is out cold, snoring like a bear, completely naked. Half of his body is plastered in red earth, the other in red wine. The front of his tent is wide open and there is cold grey stew all over his feet.

Ham takes a good long look then runs to his brothers.

'You should see Dad, he looks ridiculous!'

'What do you mean?' Shem chews on a pomegranate and eyes Ham suspiciously.

'Come see.'

Ham takes his two older brothers to the tent and stands there snorting and chuckling while they look in. Shem grabs a blanket, dusts off the dry earth and the damp food and throws the covering over his father. He loosens the tent flap and covers the opening.

Ham starts whining. 'Aw . . .!'

'You want Sara to see this? You want Miriam and Joanna? You want the kids?' Shem smacks the back of his brother's head. 'That's for being a doghead.' He slaps him again, though Ham tries to duck it. 'That's for disgracing our father.' And he slaps him one more time, this time with the other hand so he won't see it coming. 'And that's for just being all talk when it came to picking grapes.'

Ham skulks off clutching his head. Japheth aims a boot at his backside as he goes.

The two brothers look at one another and shake their heads. There was a time they'd never have dreamt of seeing this. Dad isn't what he was.

Above the skewed oak-framed door into Cutter's there's a little wooden plaque. You always have to duck down when you enter or you catch your head on it. On the left of it there's a skull and crossbones, on the right an epi-taph to an eighteenth-century Jack the Lad.

You see, Cutter was a pirate. A scar-faced rogue with an appetite for rum and bar girls. They say he had a heart of gold buried inside his tattooed chest. He would roll up here after months away pillaging and looting, choose the prettiest serving wench and spend the evening wooing her. No one knows if he actually bed-ded any of them. He seemed to just enjoy the chase. The challenge of sweet-talking another innocent. He wasn't good-looking; his eyes and his ears were too big. He had a pronounced limp from battling other pirates, and he'd mislaid three fingers somewhere along the way. But he had a certain something. A charm that he had accrued over the years and which, to this day, is legendary in the pub that bears his name.

They say he never attacked British sailors or merchant vessels. Some say he was a kind of Robin Hood of the seas. Whenever he spotted a heavily laden pirate ship alone at sea, he and his aquatic Terminators would swoop on it with a ferocity that stunned his enemies into jumping ship and leaving the booty for Cutter and his shipmates. It's said he never once attacked any other kind of vessel. Whether that's true is debatable, and of course you could still safely accuse him of profiting from other people's loss, as there are no stories of him patient-ly going round returning the treasure he found aboard these other pirate ships. But he did liberally share out his spoils with the poor of the town, casting trinkets and money here there and everywhere as he wandered the streets of an evening. Rather like Dickens sharing his stories with the illiterate, Cutter shared his treasure with the poor. He was no angel but he was admired and respected and he drank in the pub that I'm sitting in now.

But as he got older, Cutter fell from grace. He became cantankerous and selfish. Became more brutal when raiding other vessels. He boarded ships and scuppered them for no reason, and instead of wooing the young bar girls he insulted them and slapped them around in public. He stopped sharing out his wealth and hoarded it beneath the floor of a room they kept for him in the back of the pub.

Now, as I said, Cutter was no saint. But he had been highly respected. Ageing changed him though. Life wearied him and his benevolent side faded. He often drank himself into a rage and vented his anger on those who least deserved it. He lost his humour and his *joie de vivre*.

Noah, to all intents and purposes, certainly was a saint. When God looked for a man he could trust, a man who was righteous, he landed on Noah. Noah came from good stock. His grandfather was Methuselah. Now there's a name you don't hear enough of today. Meet the kids – Keanu, Cher, Brooklyn, Lourdes – and Methuselah. Shame it's disappeared as it means something pretty significant: 'When he is dead, it shall be sent'.

Now when you do the maths, it transpires that Methuselah, or Meths as we'll call him, died the same year that the flood came. Meths was nine hundred and sixty-nine when Noah was six hundred. Coincidence? I don't think so! As long as Meths was alive, he was a walking prophecy. And I guess that's why the dude lived so long. Longer than anyone else. Because God didn't want to send *it* – the flood – judgement – death – a watery grave. And the prophecy stands today. The man who lived longest stands as a reminder to us that God doesn't like sending judgement. It's not his thing. Give him a choice between death and glory – he'll always offer glory.

So in Methuselah, Noah's got a great granddad. (Not a great-granddad: that was Enoch, who was also a great great-granddad. God and he were so much in cahoots God took him away one day – voom! so they could spend more time together.) Which is another sign of how Godly this family tree is. So Noah's been brought up well. And in spite of ridicule and cynicism on the part of the rest of the known world, he gets on and builds a boat. And the rest as they say, is history. Or not depending on your theology and whether you believe there really was an ark, or just the parable of the big boat full of little animals. But that's another story altogether...

Sadly, like Cutter, Noah loses the plot a little. Like so many great men, he founders in his old age. Perhaps building that ark had been his *raison d'être*. Perhaps he spent so much of himself on that mission that he felt lost just growing a few grapes. No idea whether the drinking became a habit or not. Certainly he seemed to end up looking the worse for wear on this occasion. And his youngest boy Ham makes the most of his downfall. And Noah cursed his family as a result. That episode did not end happily.

What of the amber nectar? So many people's lives get messed up by it. So much damage, so much pain, so much squandered happiness and potential. I stare into my pint and see my face looking back, or rather a contorted version of my face, barely recognisable. That's the power of drink I guess.

Yet, Jesus made gallons of the stuff. He often hung out where there was much drinking and never once told people off for enjoying themselves. Paul prescribed wine in one letter for medicinal purposes. Jesus provided it for parties. It's so hard for us to imagine that Jesus really loved life. That he enjoyed a good time. Years of stained glass and self-flagellation have taught us that Christianity is sombre. It stands for propriety, mild manners, reserve and moderation. I doubt if the real Jesus stood for that.

Thank God for the likes of G.K. Chesterton who generally enjoyed life and said things like:

'More flies are caught with honey than vinegar.'

'If there was no God there'd be no atheists.'

And 'He is a sane man who can have tragedy in his heart and comedy in his head.' (See – www.chesterton.org/discover/quotations)

I guess Jesus had tragedy in his heart and comedy in his head, all right . . .

But back to the booze.

Clearly for many people alcohol is a bad idea – a very bad idea. But not so for everybody. I come to my pint to escape. I come to unwind, to relax. And often, I come to find a side of me that the everyday world constricts. There are bits of me that need a good loosen up.

And as for old age, well, so many of the great Old Testament leaders lose their way in their later years. They begin well, standing up for truth, dedicating their lives to God. Then, as the years roll by, they deviate and start worshipping idols. It happens time and time again. Which makes David's respect of Saul all the more remarkable. This unhinged king tried to murder him again and again, yet David chose never to harm him, and always held him in high esteem . . . even when he was dead. Unlike Ham, who takes the first opportunity to belittle his fallen father.

Old age and respect should go hand in hand. I have no idea who's really sitting there behind that old soak in the far corner of Cutter's. He coughs a lot and his tobacco smoke smells foul. He has stains down his tatty sweater and his shoes are way past their wear-by date. But for all I know he was once a hero. Maybe he pioneered major advances in medicine. Maybe he fought the Japanese in the heat of the jungle. Maybe he cared for his disabled sister for thirty-two years.

Maybe he once built a boat and used it to offer refuge to thousands of people . . .

On a beach in France.

14. Death Wish

Matthew 27:3–10

Judas stares at the rope in front of his face. It hangs like a twisting mirror, reflecting death and punishment.

Where did it all go so wrong?

How did it come to this?

He squints into the burning sky, the vultures are already gathering, swooping and circling, grabbing for bits of him like the rotting hands of the dead. He steadies himself, looks around for a rock to stand on.

Would he turn the clock back? If it were possible, would he do it? If he could start again would it really make any difference? He recalls the first time he saw Jesus; they were both in the synagogue on a dreary Sabbath. Judas had been chatting with Simon, one of the Zealots. He didn't know him, but he knew about the Zealots – revered renegades who slipped in and out of the shadows, taking Roman soldiers with them.

At that point Judas had been on the verge of becoming one of these guys. He wasn't a fighter really, spent most of his childhood ducking and diving, avoiding violence. But he was no stranger to trouble. They were the best of friends; it often came looking for him, knocking on his door, inviting him out for a bad time. As far as he was concerned the Zealots were a bunch of misguided thugs, hell-bent on anarchy. But then – something had to be done about the Romans. Simon seemed a little different, in possession of a few more grey cells than the others. They'd not been chatting long when all hell broke loose. There had been a commotion, way over in the thick of the crowd, shouts of anger and disdain, then another unusual sound – laughter. Laughter and frenzied clapping. What the heck was going on? More shouts came, blended now with insults. Then the sound of Pharisaical wrath, tunics been ripped and chests been thumped. Religious nutters. They got so chewed up about stuff that mattered so very little. An old guy appeared, pushing his way through the crowd, his face full of smiles and his hand in the air. Judas didn't know the guy from Abraham but someone shouted about a paralysed arm. Well, it wasn't paralysed now. The old jock was busy punching people's shoulders and slapping them round the face. If he hadn't just been healed someone would have decked him by now. Suddenly he was right there, grinning a toothless grin, his bad breath coming in fast guttural rasps.

'What's up?' Judas asked, backing away a little.

The old man threw just one name at him, the sound coming out with a spray of grey spit.

'Jesus!'

And then he whooped and slapped the wind out of Judas' chest then ran off to hit somebody else.

Judas stared after the dancing figure. Somewhere in the background he heard a footfall and glanced round.

And there he was.

The man with the power to put the punch back into an old man's life.

Judas had never seen him before, yet he couldn't help feeling there were something strangely familiar about this man. He wasn't tall, broad in the shoulders, legs a little blunt, chest like a mature tree trunk, hands bludgeoned from years of building work. Nothing really distinctive about him, no chiselled good looks, or fine cheek bones and he was certainly no giant of a man. There was a scar on his face, and another on his neck. The kind of jags you pick up from flying debris. But it was those eyes, clear as day. Soul windows that gleamed as if they'd been polished all morning. Eyes so open you could drive a camel through them. This was a guy with little to hide. And that was terrifying; terrifying and morbidly fascinating. Everybody's got something to hide. Judas knew that well enough. He had so many closets he could have opened a furniture store.

'Are you coming this way?'

The man smiled as he spoke, poked a thumb towards the exit. Judas must have frowned because the guy then laughed.

'Not rocket science, Judas. If you want to change the world I have a few ideas.'

So, like a little donkey, Judas padded behind this stranger who knew his name and read his mind.

You see, one thing impressed Judas that day, and it wasn't an old man with bionic fists. It was Jesus' blatant disregard for law and order. Good on you, Teacher. A bloke not scared to rattle cages and hack off a few Pharisees. Now, that's my kind of guy.

Judas never did join the Zealots. Perhaps if he had done he wouldn't now be staring up at this old bit of rope. Same bit of grizzled cord that Jesus had used on another day when he was causing more trouble . . . A week before everything went saddle over sandal, a week before the sky came crashing on their heads.

Jesus took them to the temple. When he visited places of worship he always caused a fuss. It was almost as if he went looking for trouble. Usually he was looking for sick people to heal on the Sabbath, 'cause the Pharisees hated that. They bashed on about good old man Moses and divine law and order, but they were probably just jealous, miffed that they couldn't straighten backs and bend paralysed limbs.

The Sabbath with Jesus was the greatest show in town. And this week was the best. The High Noon of all the showdowns.

Jesus took them inside, strolled about and concealed the anger brewing inside him. Then, without a word he went outside, bought a cheap bit of old rope from a market vendor and patiently sat by the road making something. Kids gathered round him and started making a game of it. What's the holy man making? A skipping rope for them? A measuring line? Something for a tug-of-war contest? Maybe a bridle for his nice donkey . . . Jesus smiled and shook his head. And the kids loved it. The disciples did their usual thing. They jockeyed for position and argued about which one of them was the coolest, or the strongest, or the wisest.

Eventually it became clear. The children looked suitably startled and the men followed him back inside. So, not a skipping rope then? No. Just a plain simple whip.

Ten minutes of slashing and slicing about, accompanied by fierce shouting and vicious accusation. Then it was all over. The house of cards had been brought crashing down. The house of prayer lay littered with broken scales and flapping birds.

Jesus stood in the middle of it, his breath coming in thick gasps, his face flushed and grim. He still clutched the rope so tightly his knuckles were white and his nails brought blood seeping through his fingers.

'Never do this again,' he hissed. 'Never take what is my Father's and use it for lining your pockets. This place is for praying. PRAYING!'

The word echoes around the upturned tables.

'Talk to God in here, don't stand there counting doves!'

And he was gone, flinging the whip to Judas as he went. Was there something in that? Something in the searing look he threw as he tossed the rope? Either way, Judas hung onto them both.

And now the memory of that look was haunting him and the rope was coming in handy.

Too many memories, too much rope.

'Look at this perfume, what a waste . . .'

'You'll always have the poor.'

'Judas, you're just a stinking thief. Stop dipping your greasy fingers into that bag . . .'

'I'll do it for thirty pieces . . .'

'Do what you're going to do quickly.'

'You betray me with a kiss?'

'I've betrayed an innocent man.'

'That's your problem.'

Was it the money? Did he really have higher principles? Messiahs don't come and cosy up to the invaders. They raise up armies, deliver earth-cracking speeches. They don't look at 1,000 crosses and just offer to be the next victim. They tear the system down, they break down the walls of heartache . . . they don't become another brick in the wall.

He looks up at the rope – one last chance to stop this. He sees the face of Jesus framed there. The man looking tired and depressed . . . that day when the crowds gave up on him because he wouldn't make magic bread for them. 'Who wants meaning? Just give us a miracle.' And the way he turned and looked at them, questions creased across his forehead.

'Look at them, leaving by the thousand. Are you guys going to follow them?'

His voice cracked a little as he asked, and Peter was quick to jump in.

'Where can we go? You're the man. You talk about eternal life – there's no one like you.'

Jesus shook his head, looked at the ground and muttered.

'Yeah, but I also picked you lot – and one you of is the devil.'

That one'll do. That rock's just about the right size. He grabs at it, hauls it off, tears off a couple of fingernails in the process. He stands on it, steadies himself. He has to adjust the rope a little, it's too low; if he put his neck in that he'd be dangling for hours, waiting for the vultures to eat him alive. That should do it. He slips his head inside. The rope feels coarse against his skin, but there's something comfortable about it too. At least the guilt will ease now, the corrosive doubts, the restless frustration and disappointment. It wouldn't be any different. Turn the clock back all you like. It was always going to be this way. Maybe he should have joined the Zealots. Jesus would be alive and he'd have been killed long ago.

He closes his eyes, steps off the rock and gags as the noose takes a stranglehold on his body.

The mood in Cutter's is sombre, and I soon find out why. Crumpled landlord offers me more than a nod and a grunt as he pours my pint. I make some chirpy, cheery comment about the grimness of the weather outside and the density of the silence inside. He says:

'Steve finished himself.'

'Sorry?'

'Steve. Topped himself. Last night in his car. Drove into his garage, shut the door and shoved a hoover pipe into his exhaust . . . £2.30.'

And that's that. Clean-cut genial guy is no more. I hand over my money in a state of shock. For the first time in my life I tell him to keep the change. There's enough there for a second pint but I'm not sure if I'll be that thirsty today. Genial guy kills himself? Why? What took him over the edge? I think back to my one close encounter with him. I have to remind myself that there was no real contact, I have no idea what was bugging him that day I saw him slouching on the bar and almost bought him a drink. Would I have made any difference? I'm about as useful as Hannibal Lecter when it comes to counselling someone; would my half-listening ear have done any good? Perhaps it was something at home. Maybe he was lonely. I remember him flicking that wedding ring. Married or not he could well have been living life in some black hole. Could have been money. He looked affluent enough, but then he looked happy too. Maybe his life was all a front. No job, no income. Perhaps his wife and kids thought he was out there selling houses when he was in here buying beer.

I flip to the demise of Judas, my pint untouched. An inglorious end for a man whose name became a byword for betrayal. No one calls their kids Judas now.

Thousands of Jews committed suicide between 1933 and 1945. Often it was only the will to live that separated those who survived from those who just couldn't see an open door ahead. The boil-infested Job wanted to die. Prayed for it. Wished he'd never been born. Pleaded to turn the clock back and sidestep that day when God wired him up in his mother's womb. But, had his prayer been answered, a hundred widows would not have seen justice, a thousand orphans would never have gained hope. Perhaps thousands more would have committed suicide if Job had never been born.

I get a vision from a scene from *It's a Wonderful Life*, the reborn George running down the high street in his home town of Bedford Falls, wishing everything and everyone an ecstatic 'Happy Christmas!' That was on the day he got his wonderful life back and Clarence the angel got his wings. But this isn't Bedford Falls and in this town you don't get your life back. Steve will always be gone now, leaving an empty space in the lives of the people who knew him and those who didn't.

Why couldn't an angel step in and stop that happening. Angels aren't just fluffy toys jammed on top of trees. They're Terminators with divine light-sabres and a strong sense of justice. Were they all on a day off when Steve fed that pipe through his car window?

I grew up believing that committing suicide was a mortal sin. Top yourself and it's a one-way ticket down below. I guess that came from Judas. Yet, if he went to hell, surely it was because he betrayed Jesus, not because he felt so much remorse that he couldn't go on.

And was it remorse? Here's this guy about whom we know so little. This shadowy angel of death who occurs every so often when there's bad news. Money gone missing from the gospel purse? Must be Judas. Prophetic perfume being spilled unnecessarily, bring on Judas. OK, so he's included on the list of the great and the good, the world famous twelve apostles, but what's his listing? Judas (who betrayed Jesus). Judas was bad news. He couldn't be trusted. He was a loose cannon.

Or was he?

Was he always out to betray Jesus? Was he always set on anarchy? Or did he start like all the others and end up spiralling downwards because of a few bad decisions?

Was his death inevitable? Was it in his genes? Was he self-destructive by nature? Was it a suicide waiting to happen? We'll never know. Maybe he really was stunned into the betrayal? Maybe he really thought he could jolt Jesus into action. Put him on trial so he could show what he was made of. But Jesus was only ever going to do that on a small scale, not on a world stage. He might reveal all to three mates on a mountain, or to a thirsty woman at an isolated well. But if he'd wanted to make a splash he'd have done it on Palm Sunday. He might have taken the opportunity to overthrow a corrupt Jewish Council, but it's unlikely he'd have done it without a few friends nearby.

But like so many well-intentioned schemes before and since – knee-jerk reactions don't make a revolution. And Jesus has already declared that his kingdom's not of this world. It's clandestine, covert, a network of spiritual spies whispering his name.

It occurs to me that I never knew Steve's name until the day he died.

And even with him gone I know nothing else. He'll be mourned by his friends and family and no doubt lamented by those of us who wish we'd known enough to stop the chaos in his head.

But most of us knew nothing. And a man who appeared to me to be genial, confident and clean cut, was clearly not. He was never a two-dimensional character. Yet I made him out to be just that. Like so many others I see and don't know.

It was once said of Charles and Diana that they were our fairytale come true, not theirs.

There are no fairytales, there's only life.

And in Steve's case today, death.

15. Proud and Prejudiced

Matthew 2

Herod is one paranoid guy. He came out of the womb looking shiftily from left to right. He's spent all his born days watching his back. He's already killed twice this month to defend his position, and now three weirdos, from some tinpot country he's never heard of, show up bright-eyed and bushy-tailed and licking their lips in search of some fabulous new monarch.

'Oh, all right. Send 'em in. Let's sort 'em out and send 'em packing. Any trouble and we'll either pay 'em off or bump 'em off. Hurry up, I haven't got all day – I'm growing old sitting here.'

They look like androgynous gnomes. Three little painted characters, faces dripping with oil and feet well-dusted from the camel ride.

'Yes? I don't have much time for uninvited guests.'

They grin like Egyptian cats.

'You invited us, your Majesty.'

Herod sighs and pushes himself out of his seat. He's been putting on weight lately and feeling decidedly unfit. He shuffles closer to the three. They stare non-plussed into his manufactured good looks.

'I hear you're looking for the king.'

One of the little elves gesticulates excitedly. He nods his head and speaks in excited chatter.

'My lord . . .'

Herod hastily corrects him. 'Your Majesty.'

'Your Majesty, we discovered a new star. Fabulous it was. We read the stars, my Lord –'

'Your Majesty.'

'– Your Majesty, and we are certain this heralds a new king.'

'But I'm the King. We don't require another. Unless you mean Caesar.' This last comment delivered with narrowed eyes.

The little elf smiles again.

'No, my Lo . . . your Majesty. We know you and we know Caesar. But this indicates an entirely different king, a new presence in the world, a new authority.'

Herod bites his lip. He towers over the three travellers.

'My authority is all that matters.'

'But my Lord . . .'

'YOUR MAJESTY!'

This time Herod bellows the correction. The three visitors fall silent. Herod turns and marches to the window. From here he can view the city. From here he is Lord of all he surveys. He thinks. He breathes deeply. He speaks again, quietly this time.

'I want to see this king for myself. You may be right, and if so, I must pay him . . .' he pauses, places his fingertips together, and says, 'what he deserves.' He turns and stares at the men. One by one they nod. 'There has been much speculation about your visit and the story you tell. I consulted with my own prophets earlier. They assure me that according to the ancient writings the Messiah must be born in Bethlehem. Maybe that's where your star will lead you.'

They nod. They don't seem to want to speak now.

'Hmm, so you believe this new king to be the Messiah?'

They nod again.

'Fascinating. And when did your star first appear?'

One of the visitors pulls a brightly decorated sack from his bag. He fishes about inside and spills a cacophony of beads and charts across the marble floor. Herod drums his fingers on the window ledge.

'Two years ago, your Majesty.'

'Two years, so . . .' Herod pauses, smiles then throws back his head and laughs wildly. There is an uncanny madness to his outburst. 'So this new king is only two years old?'

They nod.

Herod's hands tremble with exaggerated terror. 'You have me shaking in my boots.' He laughs his feral laugh again.

The travellers look at each other.

'Go!' he suddenly booms. 'Find the child, do whatever you must do and then . . .' he raises a sharp index finger, 'then come back and tell me so I may go and . . . worship him too.'

They nod, bow and shuffle off. As they go they hear the sounds of goblets bouncing off walls and a puppet king shrieking his head off.

It's Christmas in Cutter's. It's only October, but it's Christmas. On the mantelpiece above my fire a stuffed Santa is jostling for position with a plastic pumpkin. In two days he'll have the place to himself. But right at the moment it's Happy Halloween and a Merry Christmas to you all. The Santa's musical, so if you jostle him too much he starts singing a *carol*. Which *carol*? 'Frosty the Snowman'. It's not even logical. I mean, 'Santa Clause is Coming to Town', OK. Not exactly a carol, but at least it's about the big hairy bearded one. I haven't tried it but I guess that if you poke the stuffed Santa he'll probably say, 'Yo ho ho' and sing 'I saw Mommy Kissing Santa Claus'.

Bah, humbug!

I used to like Christmas. I admit I still do when I see my children happily wrecking paper and mangling boxes. (Perhaps that's where the taste for vandalism begins.) But I'm worn down now. It's all too hollow. The festivities have little lasting ring to them. I know that even before Christmas is over, the hype for the furniture sales will begin. Who wants to buy a bed at Christmas? You'd never get it down the chimney. And the much-trumpeted Double Christmas edition of the *Radio Times* is guaranteed to be bulging, not so much with good telly – but with a fat Summer Holiday supplement. Forget the horrors of the festive season – invest in a fortnight in North Korea.

When I was wee boy I used to go through this hefty tome and mark up the movies I didn't dare miss. Nowadays with 20,000 films on offer it would take me all fortnight just to do that. And I have them on video anyway. Look I'm not trying to give Scrooge a run for his money, honest. It's just that Christmas ain't Christmassy any more. *Sorry.*

Couple that with my recent discoveries that a) there was no snow in Bethlehem, b) it probably wasn't in the bleak midwinter, and c) Jesus wasn't born in a stable, and you've not got that much to put on a red suit and shout 'Yo ho ho' about. It's much more likely that Mary and Joe travelled at harvest time, when the roads had not yet been washed away by bad weather, and as the locals were pretty big on hospitality, anyone returning to the town of their birth would have had relatives there who would have gladly offered them a spare room. Depressed yet? Apparently the word 'inn' can be translated to mean 'guestroom', and you can search high and low, from Genesis to Revelation, but there's no mention of an innkeeper. There could have been cattle and sheep, 'cause they cohabited with the animals, and so Jesus would have been laid in a manger, that's bang on. But no ear-splitting crying? Come on, what winter-wonderland planet are we on here?

If you want a more gritty version of Christmas you can always watch *Die Hard* or even better turn to Revelation 12 and read what's going on behind the scenes. That happy festive tale involves a seven-headed dragon, a flying woman, an army of guerrilla angels and a life-threatening flood. Don't sing many carols about all that, do we?

Seems Christmas is far more than babies, shepherds, Santa and Frosty. It's a battle of galactic proportions, a war game where the likes of shepherds and kings are tiny characters playing out their part in a colossal set piece that will mean life and death for the whole of humanity.

And Herod, who thinks he's the king of the world, has no idea what's really going on. He's just a big man with a little influence over one or two day-to-day things. But as far as the bigger picture goes, he will be less than a gnat on the windscreen of history.

Of course, had he not been so paranoid he might have gone down in history as something other than an evil child-murdering tyrant. But like so many corrupt regimes before and since, his power corrupted him. Absolutely. Anyone who hangs on desperately to their life will lose it. The very king he was trying to destroy later said that. The tighter you grip your world, the more likely it is to buckle and explode.

Pol Pot's reign in Cambodia imploded because he began to destroy his own leaders. Any threat to the throne has to be flushed away. Other dictators have scuppered themselves on the same iceberg.

One of Jesus' great strengths was his ability to live above the temptation to grab power and hold on to it. That's what the battle in the wilderness was about. And the fruit really became evident on Palm Sunday, when the crowds clamoured to crown him King. Had he been at all insecure he would have wrapped his fists around that adulation and built an empire on it. But the very next week he's right there, kneeling before the usual suspects, washing the crud off their feet. And we discover he can do this because he's quite sure that in reality all heaven is at his command. He just doesn't need to command it.

Herod was proud and stupid, watching his own back and convinced that his happiness lay in his power – even though in reality, it was the very thing that made him unhappy and weak. He made one more mistake. He never asked any searching questions, as far as he was concerned he already had this new baby sussed. 'He's a threat. That's that.' His mind was a shut trap. Had he opened it a little he might have ended up on his knees, next to three strange men, offering a new king gold, frankincense, myrrh . . . and a first-century gift voucher. (Redeemable in all good Bethlehem stores.)

16. Getting Tooled Up

Ephesians 6:10–18

Paul painfully adjusts the shackles on his wrists. The iron's coarse and moving around too much cuts into the wounds on his arm. His ankles are bloody too. Roman chains are unforgiving. They dig deep and leave their mark. Still, that's of no importance at the moment. He's looking for a good analogy. A contemporary picture. The guys in Ephesus need to grasp what's important. It's all very well bashing on about love and prayer, but men need solid stuff, tangible examples. How can he make them see why this stuff's important? Why does it matter anyway? In a world of commerce and industry, war and trade, what place does righteousness and truth occupy?

War. Now there's a thought. He glances across at one of the guards. A vicious Spaniard with the face that launched a thousand headbutts. His nose is broken and jagged scars decorate his forehead. He's lost several teeth and an eye. But he's still faster and harder than most men who have 20/20 vision. Paul's seen what happens to prisoners who mess with him. So what would make a brickhouse like him sit up and take notice of the spiritual world?

Well, the guy likes a good fight, so better start there. It's a battle, there are two sides to the war raging round the planet – one you can see, and one you can't. OK, so how d'you fight a battle and survive?

Paul glances across again. The Spaniard is clocking him now, giving him the once over with his good eye. Paul looks away, swallows hard. He stares at the ground, subservient and quiet. He's already had one beating today, he doesn't need another. Especially not from a guy who could kill him with one blow of his jackhammer fist.

Think. There's something in this. Think Paul.

'You!'

Oh grief, I'm a dead man. Please God, don't let me die. I'm not done with living yet.

'I'm talking to you . . . missionary man.'

Paul sneaks a look. The soldier's leaning on the bars, his face pushed between the metal. The skin is stretched back over his cheeks, giving him the look of a slightly starved wolf. He grins and the gaps in his teeth show through.

'What are you doing?'

'Nothing. Thinking.'

'About what? I saw you looking. You think you can get past me?'

Paul smiles then regrets it.

'You think I'm funny? I'll show you a joke right now . . .'

'No, no I swear I have no intention of trying to break out. Look at me. How would I ever get past you?'

'Feet first.'

The soldier laughs at his own joke; Paul does his best to join in.

'Do you believe in the gods?' he asks.

The soldier shrugs. 'The gods? Why not.'

'Do you believe in truth?'

'I believe in this.'

Paul almost leaps out of his skin as the Spaniard unleashes his sword and smashes it against the bars. The sounds of violence ring around the cell, and to make the point, the soldier slashes a second time.

'But what about faith? Don't you need that? Doesn't it give you some help . . . some protection?'

'I have a whacking great shield. If I need protection I grab that. And I have this.' He smacks a rocky fist against his chest. There's the dull clunk of bone against metal.

Paul looks down at the man's feet. There's little protection there.

'Why don't you wear boots?'

'Because feet need to be fast. I don't want to protect them, I want to move them. Run rings around scumbags like you. Ah, I'm bored of this. Let me sleep. Be glad I'm tired otherwise I might beat you senseless for asking too many questions. You sleep too. Now! Sleep! Sleep! Stupid missionary man.'

Paul shuts his eyes and crouches against the cold damp stone. But sleep is the last thing on his mind. He's thinking of shields and swords and sandals. This is what he's been looking for; the Spaniard has unwittingly given him the imagery he needs.

When he asked about truth the guy swung his sword, instead of faith he wants a shield, and his feet need to be fast to keep up with the battle. Fine. That's what it is then. The guy wears a breastplate and belt too. So what else d'you need to be a man of God in this day and age? Truth and righteousness. That'll do it. You need all these things if you're gonna survive and make sense of a hard world. He sneaks a final glance but Spaniard's eye is shut. He wears no armour on his back. But then he probably never thinks about retreating.

The problem with the stuff in my little black book is, because it's in my little black book, if I'm not careful, I can revere it so much that I prevent it coming too close to me. Because it's in these hallowed pages, I can see it almost as set in stained glass. What do I mean?

Well, everything recorded on these scuffed pages originally happened in the context of life. The God of heaven is the God of *now*.

But we read about all that and set it back in gold-plated, stained-glass history. Never to be altered. But if there's one thing that matters to God it's surely the here and now. Not the there and then. He's always contemporary. Always relevant. All of this has been laid down and carefully recorded to get us through today. And anything that gets in the way of that needs addressing.

Jesus turns up and uses the media of his day. The prophets likewise.

So, if Paul uses the analogy of the Roman armour it's because the blokes in his churches are seeing soldiers all the time. We don't. I see men in suits, lads in jackets and jeans, mechanics in overalls and kids in baseball caps.

The Gospels were originally laid down in the common language of the people. Everyday language for everyday life. Only time and conditioning has turned the Bible into a book one step removed from normality. OK, so there's poetry and wisdom and psalms in there, but even so, the content of these was scribbled down to help us live, not to help us perform. This is not Shakespeare or Dickens or Homer. This is reality, and surely anything that makes it harder to apply and understand is unhelpful.

So what's the equivalent of the armour today? If Paul were emailing us from the Strangeways Internet café, and wanting to communicate a list of things that mattered, what might he use to fix it in our minds? For a mechanic perhaps it would be a set of tools. For a computer technician – a page of software. For a full-time dad with four young kids, a list of essentials from Safeway. For crumpled landlord behind the bar – a round of drinks. For the two builders – a set of tools. You get the picture . . .

Dear Dave,

Hope you're doing well, I'm stuck in prison, food's terrible, toilet stinks, and you can't bend down in the shower. Wish you were here. Oh one last thing, the world's a bad place out there so here's a few things to help you win the game. Stay fit and focused, keep practising but do it with God's coaching. Don't try and win this on your own. The game's tough out there so when you go out and step up to the crease don't expect to win if you're standing there in your pyjamas. If you don't have the necessary gear you'll be in all kinds of trouble. This match isn't against players made of flesh and blood, but against the evil bowlers and fielders of the unseen world, against those mighty wicketkeepers of darkness who rule this cricketing universe, and against those wicked umpires behind the celestial stumps.

Use every piece of God's kit to resist the enemy in this test series of evil, so that when the game ends you will still be batting there, not out. Stand your ground in front of the wicket of life, putting on the box of truth and the kneepads of God's righteousness. For good grip put on the shoes of peace, so that you will be fully prepared to stand your ground, not lose your footing, and to make those runs as swiftly as possible. In every battle you will need to wear the gloves as your protection – to deflect the knuckle-busting spinners aimed at you by Satan. Put on salvation as your visor, protect your head and your mind with the dead certainty that you're a vital part of the team, and take the bat of the Spirit, which is the Word of God. Be familiar with it, so you can use it well, and take a good stance so you can knock those fast balls for six. Pray all the time, keep communicating with the other batsman, and on every occasion don't try and win this alone. Stay alert and be persistent in your match-play, aware that you don't do this for yourself, but for all good cricketers everywhere.

Oh and if you win the toss, bat first.

Cheers,

Paul

PS Send me a cake with a hacksaw in it, will ya?

17. You Can Choose Your Friends . . .

Genesis 42 – 45

Joseph can't quite believe this.

Ten heads bow before him and it's just like a flashback.

Ten heads, ten stooping sheaves of corn. Ten men, ten subservient stars. He can't take this in. So it's come true. After all these years, it's actually come true.

He knows what he wants to say to them. He's practised it, many times. In that stinking well, in Potiphar's study, in the long nights in prison. He even scripted some of it. He didn't want to get it wrong.

They're older of course. All of them aged by time, famine and the past. How often have they thought of him? How many of them have speeches ready for him?

None. There'll be no doubt about that. Joseph's dead. Why on earth should they prepare an apology? Why on earth would they expect to be here now bowing before their younger brother, him daubed in colour, them dressed in rags? All they want is corn from this faceless official. Well, brothers, this official is in charge of the world's superpower, and right now he holds your life in his hands.

And so Joseph discovers what it feels like. What it feels like to command a brother's life. They found out twenty years ago. They failed the test. Will he?

He knows what he wants to say . . . But he won't say it. He can't bring himself to appear so vulnerable. His pride stops him from stooping low and group-hugging the lot of them. Joe's grown up – but not that much.

'Where are you lot from?'

'From Canaan, sir.'

He runs his eyes from face to face. He's hiding behind a wall of make-up. They don't have the first notion who he is.

'I know your kind. You're spies. This is a reconnaissance mission. You're planning an invasion.'

'That's ridiculous. We're just hungry. Look at all these other people. We're just like them. We're brothers, honest men.'

'Oh sure. Honest men. That's right. So how honest was that when you took my coat home after leaving me for dead.'

Of course he doesn't say that. That would be too quick and easy. He's gonna make them pay. But not for the corn.

'You want to see how vulnerable the famine has made us. Tell the truth!'

'We are telling the truth. Our father sent us to get food because we're starving in Canaan. We are twelve brothers.'

'Where are the other two, then?'

'Our youngest is back with our father. The twelfth is . . . no longer with us.'

Oh yes he is. You have no idea.

'You lie.' Joseph paces. The brothers stay on their knees. 'I want to see this younger brother. All of you will stay here, only one may return and fetch him. Which one will it be?'

'Please, sir, don't do this. Our father will not survive the trauma.'

'Which one?'

'Please . . .'

'DECIDE! NOW!'

But there's no decision. So he claps them in all prison. And it's getting out of hand.

What was that speech again, what was he going to say? When he goes home that night he is wrung out. He hunts about for the papyrus. He can't find it.

He lies down but sleep won't come. He orders a drink, then a meal. He has none of it. The dawn rises and he's sick to his stomach. This goes on for two more days. On the third day, he visits them in prison; they look like he feels.

'All right, look. I'm an honourable man. And God-fearing too. I don't want people to suffer. It's been a hard week. Listen, I will keep one of you here. The rest of you can go. Go and bring back Father . . . your father, and this other . . . what's his name? Benjamin. Yes. You, Simeon, that's your name, isn't it? I saw it written down some-where . . . You must stay.'

This is good news and bad news of course, but to the brothers it all sounds bad.

'This is happening,' they mutter in their native tongue, 'because of Joseph. God is punishing us. We heard him screaming and yelling in that well and we did nothing. We should have helped him. We murdered him.'

The guards have no idea what's going on but Joe of course knows every word. It's at this point that things overwhelm him. He staggers from the room and falls to his knees in an empty chamber. He sobs and sobs and sobs. Years of grief and pain erupt from his chest. He pours out the agony until there is nothing left. He decides to go back and tell them the truth. Enough of these games, he'll tell them who he really is. He washes, applies more make-up and returns.

But he still can't do it. When he's alone he knows what to do, but when he sees them, it's too difficult. He knows what he should say, the words are all there, but they stick in his throat. So, instead of the bear hug of brotherhood and the hand of friendship, he comes with a rope and orders that Simeon be trussed up in front of them.

'Prepare grain for the rest of them,' he tells the guards, 'and let me inspect it before they leave. Oh and don't mistreat this one. He may be in prison, but he's not to be . . . abused.'

When Joe inspects the grain he doesn't take one look at the food. He's only come to slip their money inside. This thing's spiralling out of control. He's kidnapped good old Simeon, that makes him no better than them. The least he can do is give them a rebate. If nothing else it gives them more money to buy extra food.

Time slips by. Joseph checks the hundreds of transits arriving in Egypt each day. The storehouses are holding out, they're making good profit on the grain, and before too long the famine will be over. But there is no sign of his brothers. Every time ten men bow before him he runs down, clutches the beards and lifts the heads. But they're always strangers. From time to time he visits Simeon, and they chat about the old days. Simeon has no idea that this is what they're doing, he just tells Joe about the good and bad times: About his nephews and nieces, about the years of prosperity, about the violence and the family feuding.

And when it happens, as is so often the case, it's on a day when Joseph is least expecting some familiar faces. He's in his chamber, wrestling with his sons. Manasseh has his head in an armlock, Ephraim is pummelling his stomach with fast little fists.

'We win! We win!' They're yelling, Manasseh punching the air with his free hand. Joe flips him over his head and hurls his body onto Ephraim. They both bounce off the bed and crash on the floor.

'Not this time – you little royal thugs!' he says.

'Tell us another dream, Dad.'

'Yeah, and tell us what it means.'

'It doesn't work like that, guys, you tell me a dream and I then interpret it.'

'I dreamt I was walking along and seven fat tigers came out of the Nile. They had huge fangs dripping with blood and human flesh. Then seven ugly lions came along and ate them all up. And then I ate the lions up and danced on their bones. What's that mean, Dad?'

'You ate too many figs and one day you'll be a vegetarian.'

'Really?'

'No.'

'Oh . . .'

'Sir, those men are back.'

The three of them stare at the servant in the doorway. Manasseh says, 'Dad – what men?'

'Be quiet, stay here and kill your brother.'

'Aw!'

'I mean it, this is serious business.'

The moment he sees Benjamin his chest tightens and his heart dodges a beat.

'Bring them to the palace.'

The brothers are terrified. They just wanted more grain. They've brought back double in payment along with some bulging bags of spices. They just want to go in peace. They don't need this special treatment. They just want Simeon home before the whole darn business kills their father.

Joe leaves them, collapses in his chamber and sobs again. He makes so much noise he fears the boys will come running. But they don't hear. No one hears. He just paces the carpet, gasping and clutching his chest as if he's having a heart attack.

Then Joseph throws a banquet. But no one has much appetite.

It's not clear when he dreamt up the final scheme. But he knows there's one last card he must play. He'll find out if they've changed. Will they still sacrifice a young brother to save themselves? Or do they care more about others than themselves now? This last trick will settle it one way or the other.

Turns out that the old soak in the corner has a large family. Either that or he has a diverse fan base. In spite of his hacking cough, the foul tobacco and the pronounced staining he is today surrounded by eight adults and somewhere in the region of fifteen children. For a moment I wonder if Santa Claus has come to town. But no, it's this old guy with an incredibly doting family. The children are clambering all over him and the parents are buying him drinks.

Child-repellant teacher is at the bar. He nods and informs me it's Edgar's birthday. So he's called Edgar then. He's eighty and clearly had a prolific life. Apparently he grew up around here but has only recently moved back, when his wife died. He's a war veteran and recently took part in the Remembrance Day parade in London. I guess he must have scrubbed up a little for that.

Children are gloriously undiscerning when they're little. My daughter doesn't have half the preconceptions I do. Sure she doesn't take to everybody, but it's usually because they're not wearing pink, or don't offer her enough sweets. I tend to avoid people for rather more mature reasons. Stains on the jumper, shoes out of fashion, that sort of thing.

It amuses me that Christians – everywhere – are often referred to as 'a family'. Is that idealistic, or just spot on? I'm sure most people imagine a place of endless back-patting and the freedom to play whatever music you like at whatever volume, with everybody else always on hand to wash, iron and cook for you. But in reality it's like any other family, lots of bickering, one half not talking to the other, and a constant debate about the choice of programming.

Families. Can't live with them. Can't live without them. Look at poor Joe. 'Course he wanted to do the right thing. 'Course he wanted to hug 'em all and spring a neat happy reunion on them . . . a few streamers and a cake with a girl inside. But, it's one thing to plan what you're going to say. It's quite another to execute it when you meet them in the flesh. I always want to tell people I care about them and I think they're great – but when they're standing there right in front of me with all that history and their hair annoying me, and the TV too loud, well it all goes pear-shaped.

Jesus has the same problems. He wasn't immune to family struggles. His mum, bless her, tries to kick start his miracle-working at the wedding at Cana.

'They've run out of wine, this is your chance!'

'Easy, Mum, I'm a big boy now.'

And of course, like so many of us, when he thinks about his mum's advice, he reconsiders, and says to himself, 'Ohhh, it was a good idea, wasn't it?'

And then the time when he's out there, busy doing his stuff, involved in miracles and teaching, the crowd hanging on his every word. And suddenly, boom, reality breaks in.

'Jesus, your mum's outside. Can she have a quick word?'

Perhaps he'd not been home lately, perhaps she was hoping he might drop by, perhaps she was cooking his favourite dinner that night. Whichever, Jesus feels compelled to use the incident to illustrate the kingdom.

'Who is my mother, who is my family? Everyone can be. Anyone who hears my words and obeys them.'

Did that hurt his mum? Did he later go and see her? Was he embarrassed by his family's presence? Did it seem inappropriate to him? I can't help wondering these things. Of course, I'm sure that whatever his response it involved no sin, but it might still have upset his nearest and dearest.

We always hurt the ones we love, don't we. It's so easy to do. This familiarity dogged him at an earlier time when he began doing stuff in Nazareth and the locals recognised him and said,

'Hang on, this is just young Jesus. He's not the Messiah, he's just Joe's boy.'

The local boy couldn't make good.

Edgar's family are drifting off. Two of the men, they look like his sons, have gone to play pool. A couple of the older grandchildren, daughters in *Hollyoaks* T-shirts and rainbow jeans, have gone to change the music on the juke box. Two of the toddlers, a ginger-haired brother and sister, are still bouncing on Edgar's knee but the rest have either gone to the toilet or gone to sleep. The two ginger ones are giggling and spilling crisps on his trousers, but let's face it, it makes little difference . . . to Edgar or his clothes. Through the window I can see three of the woman arguing. Definitely a family gathering.

Of course it was never going to be easy for young Joseph. He was always a bit of a loner, he was always a bit strange. He has leadership skills and weird dreams. He doesn't fit in with the rest of the family. Most leaders don't. He probably desperately wants to fit in, but he'll always be an outsider, and even more so now that he's a world leader. Even a cool multi-coloured parka won't turn him into one of the lads now.

'We Are Family' by Sister Sledge comes on the juke box. Edgar's granddaughters giggle and boogie to it. Wouldn't be a bad song for Christendom except that it features the line about having all your sisters with you. Still, sums up much of the church I s'pose. I prefer the raw *Kings of the Wild Frontier* by Adam and his Ants – he sang about a new kind of royal family, a nobility running wild. Pretty sure Paul talked about royalty in his letters.

It's time I ventured back to my family, I have visions of toddlers banging on the pub door asking for daddy. That won't do. Not at all. I close the book and down the pint. Sometimes there are just no straight answers in the Bible. You just have to read and observe, and hope you don't make the same mistakes some of these heroes made.

18. Moses the Murderer

Exodus 3 and 4

Moses gets stiffer by the day. You'd think that a man who's spent forty years on the move would stay supple forever. But no. It's the price you pay for getting old. Age never comes alone. Always comes with a few mates. Insomnia, incontinence, poor eyesight and diminishing sex drive.

The sheep drive him up the wall these days, his irritation swelling with his waistline. Disappointment is the main problem. Life just didn't work out the way he expected. Forty years in Egypt spoilt him rotten. For too long he had his cake and ate it. Those days seem like a dream now, a dream that became a nightmare that became a slow lingering death in the desert heat.

Where are the wine and roses? The status and the stardom? What happened to the perfumed dancing girls and the royal harem? His wife drives him mad too. Somewhere deep down he knows that he'd never find a better woman, never have what they have if he was with one of the Egyptian girls. He never met anyone like Zipporah when he was swanning around the royal court. They understand each other, they laugh at each other's jokes and foibles, they shoot from the hip and speak from the heart. But there's no danger. No mystery. No chase. The exquisitely perfumed Egyptians satisfied his every need. Zipporah won't play that game. Romance left this building a while ago. Marriage has bred contempt.

She knows, of course, about the skeleton. The one buried back there in the shadow of the pyramids. She's always accepted him for it, never brought it up, never used it as ammunition. She's always comforted him when he's woken on those cold nights, doused in sweat with his teeth and fists clenched. He fled the past, but the past won't flee him; it clings like a bad smell.

Yet he was only doing the right thing. You see an armed man beating the living daylights out of a malnutritioned woman, what else are you gonna do? Stand back and buy a ticket? His anger still rises when he recalls the next part. That moment when he tapped the soldier on the back of the neck, raised the spade, slapped the soldier's face with the underside and then proceeded to smash his head to a pulp. He wasn't just revenging this woman, this moment was for every man, woman and child he'd seen beaten and starved by a regime that bore his name. The horrified slave stared wide-eyed as he went on, cracking metal on bone, again and again and again until the body twitched no more and there was just a grey-pink mush where the head had once been. As he threw down the weapon, he had tried to smile at her to reassure, but his brutality had shaken the girl to the core. She turned and fled like a crazed animal, spewed the story to the others in her work detail. And the next day Moses had been the one doing the fleeing.

The sheep bring him back to reality. They're bleating about something. Stupid beasts. What now? It's just another thicket on fire. You see them all the time. Bushes always go up round here, it's the heat and the lack of water. Where is his flask? Oh there. He trudges across towards the bush, bends to pick up the canister. OK, so that is odd. The thing's on fire but nothing's happening to it. No charring of the wood, no splintering twigs. How does that work then?

Oh. Was that a voice?

Moses spins round, expecting some kind of raiding party. Sheep have been disappearing lately. You have to keep watch. No good shepherd falls asleep on the job . . . But there's no one. He must have imagined it . . .

'Moses.'

OK. That was real. That was . . . The bush?

He can't tell if the sheep can hear the voice or not. They're just milling around as ever. No alarm, no interest. Just the usual hunting for a better class of grass. Moses moves up to the bush. He stops. He removes his sandals. He falls like a rock and pushes his face into the hot sand.

So this is the end then. This is what he's feared for so long. God's come looking for him about the murder. It's payback time. You don't meet God and live. This is a one-way ticket to the world of the dead. Any minute now his heart will freeze and the jackals will take away his body piece by piece. What will happen to Zipporah? What about his son?

'Moses, get up. I have a job for you. My people are suffering and dying in Egypt. I've come to do something. I'm going to move them to a land dripping with goodness. A land oozing with opulence.'

Moses stands, his eyes full of stinging sand. He can barely see now, but there's no doubting the voice. He checks his body. As far as he can tell, he's still alive.

'Moses, are you listening?'

'Oh sure. Great idea, don't know why you didn't step in sooner . . .' He can't understand why he's not dead.

'Well, I'm stepping in now. But you know, I never do things alone. So . . . it's your time – go.'

'Great idea, get them out of there the quicker the be . . . Sorry?'

'Off you go. Pack up. Get back to Egypt.'

'Me? ME? No that's not a good idea. I'm still on their wanted list back there. There are most likely still a trail of wanted posters from here to the Sphinx. Anyway – I tried that forty years ago. I wished you'd shown up then, I wanted to change things then. Not now. I'm too old now. You should try the job centre.'

'I'll be with you, Moses. Don't worry about your age or your past. When you set them free, bring them to this mountain and worship me.'

'Listen. Who am I? Some old lag who got adopted by the royals and then scarpered. If I go to the Israelites and do this – why are they going to listen to me? I can tell them, "God says this, God says that" – and they'll say, "Oh yeah? Fascinating. Which God is this, then? The God of convicts?"'

'Moses – just tell them I am who I am. If they want more detail, mention their ancestors. It's the same God, Moses. The One and Only. Now, here's the plan, get all the leaders together. Tell them about this meeting, tell them I know life has been bleak for them, but the future's bright. Then take them to Pharaoh. Don't just demand he sets everyone free. That won't work, tell him you want three days holiday to take the Israelites into the desert to worship me. Now, Pharaoh will of course refuse so that's when you can do a few miracles and Egypt will be running round like a scalded sacred cat for a while.'

'Hang on, you're saying I go to Pharaoh, demand a long weekend for everyone – even though you know he'll refuse? Right. OK, look, I won't even get that far.

The Israelites won't believe I've seen you. They haven't see you in years, why should I have the privilege? Hmm?'

There's a noise from the bush that's not unlike a long-suffering sigh.

'Right. What's that in your hand? A staff. Well done. Throw it on the ground. Just do it, Moses! Why do you have to argue all the time? Thank you. See, *voilà*, a snake. Believe me – they'll believe you when they see that. Scratch your chest a minute. Yes, now. Now take your hand out. Don't worry, it's just leprosy. You look a bit pale, stick it back in your tunic. See, gone! Are you impressed yet? You know how the Egyptians love the Nile and reckon it's such a sacred thing? Well, when you dip your staff in and turn it into the biggest blood bath in the world, they'll have a bit of a wake-up call. Then after that…'

'Look, I'm sure they'll be well-chuffed with all this magic. Sorry, miracles. But that's not the point. I can't stand up in front of people and spout lots of rhetoric. I leave that to the priests and the politicians. I'm an action man.'

'I know that, I've seen you in action. But you forget – who made your mouth? Who put that tongue in your stubborn head? Moses, it's not pyramid design, me! Yes, I should know what I'm talking about.'

'*Look – how many times do I have to say this? I don't want to do this! I have a wife and family, I'm old and tired. Send someone else!*'

'*You think you can shout, Moses*? WELL, LISTEN TO THIS!!'

The ground trembles for a moment. Moses backs away from the bush. He has a headache by now. The desert falls silent. Has God gone? Is he summoning the angel of death to swing his sword?

'OK, your brother Aaron. Remember him?'

Moses wipes his forehead. 'Yeah – he's a good speaker. Send him.'

'Absolutely.'

'Thank you.'

'He's going with you. Don't start, Moses. Don't start. Just pack your bags and go meet your brother, he's on his way right now. Tell him the plan, and I'll keep you both informed. Off you go. Off you go! Er . . . Moses. Nice talking to you. And Moses . . . Don't forget your staff . . .'

It's lunchtime on a drizzly Monday and the place is deserted. Just me and the landlord.

I ask him for my usual and after a moment's thought he grunts and recalls it. I'm hardly a regular. Once a fortnight if I'm lucky. If I was a regular he'd be on the street selling *The Big Issue*. I've got a nerve really asking for *my* usual. I ask him about Stacey and he eyes me suspiciously, I'm disclosing my penchant for people-watching. Oh all right – call a spade a spade – I'm nosy. I watch and listen. I get nothing out of him regarding his daughter, but then why should I? As far as he's concerned I'm just another customer getting my hopes up.

I ask him about Cutter's. I wonder how long he's been here. Eighteen years. Before that he was in another pub in another town. Does he enjoy it?

He raises a bushy eyebrow, looks at me as if the question's daft. Eventually he shrugs and tells me it's what he does.

I take my pint and run. It always happens like this. I start out feeling this strange compulsion to interact with other people then end up retreating and feeling bad.

'Brought your book, then?' he mutters from the bar, as I pull out my Bible.

I nod sheepishly. I'm not the only one who *people watches*, then.

I have a soft spot for Moses. He's a genuine, honest, caring guy. Battered by life and disappointed at the way things turned out. I've no idea what he expected, but looking after sheep in the desert wasn't on his 'To Do' list.

That's why he's so shocked when God shows up.

Notice a few things here. We have no idea if he was a spiritual guy. We don't know if he prayed much, there's no record of him worshiping or sacrificing. All we know is that life started out well and ended badly. He literally had a charmed existence. On the extermination list at birth he was scooped to safety by a princess and returned by *accident* (God's anonymity at work) to his real mother. Then he lives high on the hog for forty years. That's when it all falls apart. From privileged prince to fugitive murderer in the space of twenty-four hours. How unlucky can you get? It's almost as bad as Lot choosing Sodom for a place to raise his family.

Now, another forty years later, this guy's broken. He's had all the life squeezed out of him and he just wants to fade away and die. You'll be lucky. Moses has a power-pack of potential stuffed away inside him. He doesn't know it but he's been training for forty years . . . longer – all his life.

'Moses, I need a bloke who understands the workings of the Egyptian court. Any ideas? I need a guy who has relatives in the Jewish quarter. Any suggestions? Oh, and I need a dude who understands the desert as I have a load of sheep I want leading across. Know anyone?'

And the more Moses argues with the Creator of the universe, the more God must have been thinking, 'This guy's gonna be great! If he isn't afraid to tell me the truth, talking to Pharaoh's gonna be a doddle. He won't be phased by the pomp, he won't by cowed by his authority. He'll tell it like it is. Whatever I ask him to say, however tough, he'll say it. Moses, whether you like it or not. You got the job.'

You see, Moses wasn't picked because he was a good disciple. He wasn't picked because he was spiritual. He was picked for that job because of his personality and his life experience. And in spite of the rocky start, he and God became the best of friends.

It's an amazing tale, and a relationship never to be rivalled. In an age way before the coming of Christ, Moses and God had an intimate friendship. They wrestled, haggled, debated and discussed. This wasn't just a friendship of convenience. This thing went deep. Moses' prayer life wasn't just please, thank you and sorry, as mine is. In a way it wasn't even prayer. It was genuine, raw communication.

My guess is crumpled landlord is doing what he does best, pouring pints. For all his bluff and gruffness, he's at home there.

Like Moses.

Everyone's been designed to do something. The trick is finding that, and having the courage to say 'yes', when everything inside of you is yelling 'no'.

19. Cross-carrying for Beginners

Matthew 10 and 16

Jesus pushes the hair from his eyes and spits in the sand. There are streaks of mud on his fingers. Behind him, in the distance, a blind girl is still wiping the muck from her face. Only she's not blind any more, and she'll take that muck home and treasure it forever.

'Lambs among wolves. Not exactly a word of encouragement, is it? But I didn't come to make you nice. I didn't come to make life free and easy. It doesn't work like that. Out there . . .' He points wildly and his arm spins and swirls like a sabre. 'Out there you have to have your wits about you. Be like snakes. Yeah, snakes. The shrewdest of all animals. Be wily and subtle and patient. A snake'll wait for hours to strike. And be like doves. Yea, I know, some snakes eat doves; and you'll be tempted to devour one another. But have goodness in your soul. Whatever you do, do it with kindness. Let humil-ity be the music playing in the background. Don't be sheep, don't be gullible. But be caring. And be men of peace. Don't go cursing any villages just because you don't like the look of the locals. And there will be times when you want to lash out. Some people will hate you, they'll slander you, gossip, make your life misery. You'll end up in all kinds of trouble and it won't be your doing. But any situation can be used by God, never think he's reluctant to get involved. He always wants to help, you don't have to twist his arm, he loves to muck in with you. He will be right there, giving you what you need. Strength, honesty, courage, compassion. For your part, do what he loves. Be just, be kind, be humble.

'A pupil is no greater than his teacher. You can bet that what happens to me will come to you. I've often been lonely, misunderstood, mistreated, misquoted. But there will be the good things too. I'm telling a few of you these things. You will have the ability to tell thousands. And remember, never lose sight of the truth at the heart of things. Your God cares. He cares so much he knows every hair on your head, the colour of your eyes, the length of your fingernails. Everything begins and ends with that fact. God cares for you. Nothing else matters more. And no one can take that away. Miracles will come and go. Friends will arrive and desert you. Family may surround or abandon you. Governments may rise up and kill you. You'll lose things, break things, forget things and outgrow things. Nothing can take away the love of your God. No one can get to that. They can suck the life from your body, but they can't get within spitting distance of your soul.'

He pauses, walks to the nearby well, and flicks water on his face. The guys watch him. They're never sure with Jesus; has he finished yet? He holds up a handful of water, it spills as he offers it to them, the drops making a spattered line in the dust at his feet.

'There are plenty of good things on offer. Give a cup of water to a thirsty soul and you'll get a bonus. Listen carefully to those who speak with authority. Recognise and respect the good and the Godly. Do all this as if your life depended on it.'

He waves at them and gestures towards a nearby carpenter's shop. He walks over, reaches for a hammer and lifts it with a distant look in his eyes.

'Be honest in your work. Honour God in your business deals. Do your best not to cheat.' He holds the hammer up and points the head towards the road snaking out of town. 'Take up your cross. Bin your selfish ambition. On a daily basis if you have to. Too many men have destroyed themselves chasing after what they cannot keep, losing the very thing they were searching for. If you live for yourself, you'll atrophy. Your soul will grow listless, your conscience will slip into a coma. You'll become a walking vegetable. Gain the whole world and you'll struggle to find yourself. Lose the world and you'll find what you were looking for when you went looking for the world. Give up your life and I guarantee you'll find it. Shoulder that cross, and follow me.'

His hand still holds the hammer, and the hammer still points to the road. A number of crosses line the way. Some of the criminals are still alive, squirming, twitching, gasping for their last breath. Jesus puts down the hammer and leads the disciples out of town and past the dying men.

It's not fair. I've not been in Cutter's for months. Well, two months. Almost. But it feels like a lot longer. The family has been ill, diarrhoea has ravaged them. It's gone through them like a ton of brown runny food. Our toilet has been like Niagara Falls. Work? Work? Don't ask me about work. That's been more stressed than the suspension bridge. Those above me breathing fire, those below me dropping like dead leaves. And talking of breathing fire, the in-laws have been to stay for an extended period. They haven't seen the grandchildren for a while. I usually offer them my children as a take-out affair, rather than an eat-in. In fact, I'd be very happy to rent 'em out for a few weeks. Rent? I'd pay.

But now we're over it all, sickness and in-laws are a thing of the past and normal chaos has been restored. And I'm wrung out. So I slipped out for a slow one at Cutter's. I grab a Guinness and reach for my black book. Drat. It's not there. It's not there! I check all my pockets. Twice. Even that little one at the top of your jeans that you never use for anything except fluff and biscuit crumbs. I'm black book-less. That shows what carnage has come our way. I'm sitting in the pub naked. I know that's normally what I find myself doing in a dream, but I'm talking spiritually naked. All I can do is rack my brains for a nugget from last week's church.

'Take up your cross.'

There's one. And 'Go in peace.'

That's my favourite bit.

You see, life has been so out of sync I even managed to get to church on Sunday, or rather I didn't manage to get *out* of going. With the extended family present and attending, apparently it would have seemed odd for me not to be part of the picture. If you ask me, it was spectacularly odd for me to be *in* the picture.

'Take up your cross.'

Jesus was uncompromising, wasn't he? Why couldn't he have just made it a little more attractive? Take up your cross, for a few yards or so. Till the end of the street. Till you feel a bit tired. Take up your cross, and put it down again. Do some exercises with it. And up and down, and up and down, and rest. Take up a little cross, a fluffy cross, a chocolate cross. A happy cross. A little cross of calm.

What must it have been like for him talking about crosses anyway? Did he know by then that there was one in the store out the back with his name on it? Surely he must have done. It would have been cruel coincidence if he didn't. Of course he knew. So where did the courage come from to talk about it so freely?

He'd probably seen many crosses. And not in people's ears, but real, with the bodily fluids still dripping off them. Interesting that he never protested about the injustice and the tyranny of it all. When people tried to engage him in political debate he took them on another course.

When news came that Pilate had slaughtered some Jews as they worshipped, instead of using the opportunity to insult the Romans, he turned the news around. Jesus seemed to think people were convinced it was some kind of punishment, so he assured them it wasn't.

'You're all sinners and need to get things sorted out with God,' he said.

And if this didn't make the point he referred to another news item. The death of eighteen people killed in a freak accident at Siloam.

'Were they being punished?' he asked. 'No. You all need to get your lives sorted with God.'

Perhaps he guessed that they were hoping he'd diss the Romans. But he wouldn't engage in that kind of political arm-wrestling. Or maybe he just knew that when bad things happen we naturally assume we've done something to cause them. Or we want someone else we can blame.

So, in an age of electric chairs and life sentencing, what does cross-carrying mean anyway? One thing's for sure, it doesn't necessarily mean dying for the faith. For some of the first followers, it clearly did, and sure, the last century may have seen unprecedented numbers of martyrs, but the history of Christendom proves that many, many Christians ended their days with a cup of cocoa and a 'Sleep well, see you tomorrow . . .'

I'm also assured that it doesn't mean being a doormat. Even when Jesus spoke of turning the other cheek he did not mean, be a walkover. Apparently turning the other cheek was a defiant gesture, not a subservient one.

The Christian side of life is certainly not going to be easy. It will cut against the grain. We all know that. It becomes complicated when we deliberately go looking for it to be hard. When we become deliberately belligerent or abrasive in regards to our faith. We can bring persecution on ourselves. I remember hearing a group of people doing some street evangelism, and their opening message was, 'Death is the perfect statistic, because one out of one people die.'

It's true – but is it the *good news*? We can make the cross-carrying heavier than it need be.

I'm not saying it should be beer and skittles, although beer and skittles can be a great night out and a chance to chinwag with people who wouldn't be seen dead in a church. Or rather, that's the one time they would be seen in one.

Clearly taking up the faith makes life more complicated and sets you apart. And the worst thing we can do is present the narrow road as some fast-moving roller-coaster ride. Pretty often it's boring and tiring and fraught with difficult moral decisions. And having to clear up diarrhoea. Let's face it much of the Christian life is just real life. But Jesus also called us to be salt for society, and salt is good, tasty and stops things going stale.

As I pick up my tired body and brace myself to return to the battlefield of toddlerdom, I recall one other thing. Jesus was clear about these difficult bits of his theology in the daylight, like me, but how difficult did he find it in the dark? Not long before his death he told his mates what was going to happen, and when they tried to make it all cosy and nice he berated them. But in the dead of night, when he's alone in a shadowy garden, he *knows* he must die, he *knows* it will change the world . . . he *knows* he'll be separated from God. And if there's any way to avoid this cross-carrying, he'll take it. There isn't, so he accepts it, the faithful Son trusting the Father.

But he understands that crisis of faith. He knows we can bluster about courage and warfare with our mates, and he knows we can feel small and afraid when we're left alone with just our fears . . . and our God.

20. Enduring Little Children

Matthew 18:1–6; 20:24–28

The disciples are doing what they do best. Arguing. Jockeying for position.

'Why are you the rock, anyway? I don't get it.' James weighs a craggy stone in his hand and hurls it into the sea. 'Can't think of anyone less like a rock than you. Unless he's talking about the state of your brain, in which case solid boulder well sums it up.'

'Well, I know why you're a son of thunder. All mouth and tunic. All hot air and big noise. Let's nuke this city. Let's have the best seats in heaven . . .'

Judas laughs, he's balancing a pile of coins on one elbow.

'I don't know what you're complaining about,' he says, 'at least you're not stuck with a label like Thomas the doubter.'

'I am not a doubter.'

'Oh, come on. You wake up in the morning and want proof that it's a new day.'

Thomas shrugs; he's always kept himself to himself.

'Matt's as bad,' says Judas. 'Never trust a tax collector.'

'At least I don't steal from the petty cash.'

'You don't need to, Matt, you get your money from the Romans.'

'And what's that mean?'

'Well, you're the mathematical shyster, you work it out.'

'He can't,' James chips in, 'he's as intelligent as he looks.'

'Why do I stay with you lot? You never listen to a word he says,' mutters Matt.

'Who says?' asks Peter.

'Exactly.'

'Excuse me, it wasn't you he took up the mountain to meet Moses last week.'

'No, and it wasn't me that sank in that water.'

'No, you were the one crying like a baby.'

There's a sickening crunch as Matthew smacks Peter. Peter inevitably punches back and the two of them end up on the ground, Peter grinding Matt's face into the dirt.

'Leave him, Pete,' says Mary, 'he's not worth it.'

James jabs a finger at her. 'Stupid woman, keep out of this.'

Mary slings a bag of food at him. 'Don't talk to me like that.'

'Well I doubt if boulder-brain here needs your help against a weak string of locust urine like Matt.'

A muffled cry emerges from underneath Peter. 'I am not weak . . .'

'Well, get up then,' says James.

'He can't,' says Peter, with satisfaction.

'Let him go, Pete,' Mary tells him.

'Mary,' says James, 'I'm telling you, leave 'em alone.'

She slaps James across the face. He raises a fist but Thomas grabs it, the knuckles barely an inch from her eye.

'Go on,' she spits, defiantly. 'Hit me. Show us what a real holy man you are. Hypocrite.'

'I'm not a holy man. Never will be.'

There's more scuffling on the floor and a flushed Matt somehow crawls out from under Peter. 'Leave her,' he splutters.

'Don't defend me!' says Mary.

'Well, you were defending me!'

They're on the verge of an all-out scrap by the time Jesus shows up. He sits on a rock for a while, watching the same old scene. They never move on. Same old insults, same old egos. He eventually steps in after Mary's decked James with a right hook.

'Morning!'

They stand up straight, as if the headmaster's just walked in. Mary wipes a trace of blood from her fist. James checks his jaw for breakage.

'I see you're having a mature debate here.'

'It was him!' Several voices say the same thing while people point at different culprits.

'Whatever . . .'

Mary steps forward. 'Jesus, you settle this for us, once and for all. We just want some kind of pecking order. Which one of us is the most important? Is it John? You're always chatting privately to him.'

Jesus is not alone. He's brought a three-year-old girl with him. Her mother's nursing a baby not far away.

'You see this child? This is the best example I can give you. Learn from her, watch her, grow like her. You know something? You never have to teach a child to jump, or dance, or play, or sing or draw, or design and build things. It comes naturally. Stop all this vying for power – it's what other people do. Turn from that and learn from this.'

The girl is squatting in the dust and is piling stone upon stone. She sings tunelessly as she does this. The tower collapses and she laughs loudly. She takes another rock and begins making random patterns in the sand.

'You know, you don't have to twist God's arm. He's pleased to work with you, he's happy to spend time in your life. He loves it. And as for your ongoing battle to be the greatest, to be honest, the greatest one among you is the one who can serve and not mind. The one who can put others in the spotlight. The one who can create and not fear to fail. The one who can risk and not worry about ridicule. Come into the kingdom as you are, with your strengths and weakness, happiness and sorrow. Bring these like any child brings their mess into your home. That's how to be great. Be yourself, and be humble. Watch the children, learn from them, and when you do that, you're watching and learning from me.'

The disciples look confused. Mary frowns. No one looks satisfied. The girl leaps up, gives one of her stones to Jesus and runs off to her mother to demand some food.

'And don't ever . . . whatever you do . . . steal the innocence from a child like this. Capitalise on it, but don't destroy it. If you do that, it would be better if you were dead.'

It's not exactly great news, is it?

I'm sure the two builders at the bar, who are currently on their third pint and arguing about shotguns, will be overjoyed to learn they're supposed to become like little kids. OK, so right now they are acting like a couple of eight-year-olds, one of them's threatening to shove his peanuts down his mate's trousers, but I still don't think it will endear them to Christianity.

Did the disciples become more childlike?

Ten of the first twelve disciples died gruesomely for their faith. One took his own life and the other ended up imprisoned on an island. That's not exactly what you'd plan for your kids, is it?

Do I really have to sing songs about wise and foolish men while I watch puppets and draw pictures of whales with broken crayons? Is that what Jesus had in mind?

There's a Lego table in Cutter's. It's tucked away in a gloomy corner along with the booster seats and high-chairs. I played on it once with my son. At first we just made squares and houses, but it all got that much more interesting when we started building towers and knock-ing 'em down again. Got noisy too. There's a giant Jenga set out in the beer garden. Why do they call them *beer* gardens, by the way? It always gives me a vision of gal-lons of Stella Artois stagnating in huge greasy puddles surrounded by wilting rose bushes and half-cut lapping Labradors. Now that would be reassuringly expensive.

The Jenga's great entertainment as it always ends up with the competitive dads squeezing out their sobbing children so they can outdo one another with a tower that rivals the Empire State building. Then it all comes crash-ing down and it takes ten minutes to pull out two three-year-olds and a drunk Labrador.

But I digress. Back here by the fire I thumb these fac-tory-tattered pages – designer stressed – and wonder. OK, if I come clean and admit that I don't want to be a five-year-old again . . . What useful lessons are there in here for a guy who loves punk rock and Indiana Jones?

Ah. A breakthrough. There are a couple of things I have learnt from my two little children. Male or female you can guarantee one thing – kids don't like church. You spend most of their born days trying to encourage them to chatter away happily. Not in there you don't. Kids in church should be seen and not heard. They can't stand it. They want to be out somewhere where they can shout and sing and give up the whispering for good.

Point two. They're not humble. Anything they see, my kids want it. Even if it's mine. Especially if it's mine. 'Humility' is not my son's middle name. 'Danger' is, if the truth be told.

And now that I'm in my stride – children argue, regularly, with me and each other. They speak their mind, foist their opinion on you. They can be difficult about the simplest things.

And they're violent. They boot you in the shins, the head and the essentials. Sometimes their hitting out knows no bounds. They let you know when they're angry.

I'm not much one for this whole *mother* God thing, thanks, but when our first one popped out – or rather, when she didn't just *pop out*, it made me think. It was like squeezing solid concrete from a toothpaste tube. There was much pain, screaming and sewing up afterwards.

My wife risked her life, gave up her body for nine months, and now, she always knows where the little Exocet missiles are.

That's three things I can hold my hand *down* to. The toughest things I had to do were make birthing backing tracks which we never used, bacon and banana sandwiches we never ate, and the right noises at the right time (which helped no end I'm sure and wasn't supposed to include swearing at the midwife).

When they were babies, if I happened to end up with the little cuties in my arms it wasn't long before I'd given them away to the nearest stranger.

Even now if I'm in charge I have no idea where the little terrors are. Bombing Bin Laden for all I know.

Some dads are great. They're naturals. I'm sure that Yuppie throwback over there is brilliant with his fourteen kids. He probably tag wrestles the boys, does the make-up for the girls, and then takes his wife a banquet in bed. All before escaping to Cutter's for a lager with a slice of lime in the top.

But I'm not like that. Domesticity is a foreign country to me. Incomprehensible felt-tipped drawings and jigsaws that come in two pieces quickly lose their fascination. I want to do my own thing. Family fun is a bit of an oxymoron for me. I don't want to hang around garden centres discussing crazy paving, I don't want to pet endless guinea pigs and feed stick insects, I hate healthy long walks, and I definitely don't want to spend two hours in a draughty building on a Sunday morning singing about Jesus wanting me for a sunbeam.

Just like a kid, then.

21. It's Not All Work, Work, Work

Genesis 1

Day one. Blank canvass. Nothing happening yet again. Finally fished out the plans. I've been putting this off too long. If I don't do something about this, no one else will, no good waiting for someone to take the initiative. Let's face it, there is no one else. Created a switch and flicked it down, what I've decided to call the *on* position.

Bingo. It works. Light came on. Darkness a thing of the past. Until I flicked the switch up, what I've chosen to call the *off* position. *On off, on off.* Works a treat.

Spent the rest of the day messing about with the light. *On, off, on, off, on, off, on, off* . . . I think you get the picture. Pretty impressive. Showed the others. They like it. Especially good for things like, Sardines or Murder in the Dark. Only problem is, when you put the light out and everyone hides, the universe is so vast it takes forever to find anyone. Eventually gave up and went for a lie down. Left the light on though, it's a low energy bulb and not expensive to run.

Day two. Got out the paint pots and started work on the sky. Used about 43 billion pots of Blue Silk. Hope we have enough left for a second coat. Looks good though. Inadvertently created a thing called *The Horizon* while we were at it. Spent a long time trying to reach it to straighten it out a little as there's a bit of a camber, but the further we ran over the water, the further away it got. Gave up again and went for a swim instead. Thought we might call the waters *sea*. It's a bit boring at present but we've had ideas about making some waves. I reckon that with a bit of board and maybe a sail you could get up some speed on that stuff. Need a wetsuit though. Bits of that water are colder than Christmas. Haven't yet invented Christmas, and won't be needing that for a good while, so don't ask about it.

Day three. OK, got busy today. Made a whole load of dry land out of some of the water. Got a rotivator from a reliable source and churned over about twenty thousand miles of it. Broke for some lunch, pan-fried quatzers, with dry-roasted shmacks and manna toast on the side, and when we got back we sowed a whole load of trees, plants and grass seed. Especially like one plantation we've nicknamed 'Barbados'. Plenty of palm trees there and the dry land is a soft sandy substance where it meets the water. Ate some coconuts and pineapples and went for more swimming. Also came up with an idea for something called 'beach volleyball'. Actually, that was just the start of it. Once we got a list going we came up with a hundred different sports and games. Two hundred, a thousand. So many things you can do on sand! Not sure that 'beach billiards' will ever catch on, but we'll see. No good books around to read yet so we wrote a few.

Day four. Created night. That's basically when we flick the switch to *off*. If you want the other setting, that's called *day* and you need to switch the light on. Pretty simple to operate. Installed a timer and a few special effects, shooting stars, comets and the like.

Also made a whole lot of other lights – the stars and the moon. And a great ball of fire I've called the sun. The heat that thing gives off is awesome. Should keep the place equipped with warmth and light for a good few millennia. The moon shows up when the light's off and provides reflected glow for half the planet. You see, one half has day while the other half has night . . . I'll write it down in more detail sometime. The moon has quite an influence on the water; the wave effect created should keep any future surfers happy. We strolled on the water for a while and made another list of sports and believe me, there's a lot you can do with a bit of wood and some waves.

Day five. Sat on a rock and stared into a lake for a long time this morning. So tranquil, so still, but a little empty too. Felt the need for something called 'fish'. Slippery scaly things that might well taste good pan-fried. So I put 'fish' on the 'To Create' list and then had to add 'birds' because Gabriel's been out and bought a pair of binoculars. Actually he didn't *go out* as such. He bought them on the uni-net, the great galactic grid. Or the 'ggg' as we like to call it. There's a junior cherub who promises delivery the next day or your money back.

So today was all about sea monsters and flight paths. Made truckloads of tropical fish and electric squiggly things, but my favourite's something I think might finish up being called Leviathan. Huge creature. Spent a lot of time on various birds, so much so that we ran out of time on this thing that looks a real dodo. That one may never actually get off the ground. Heard some sneezing as we left them all to it. Hope they're not prone to contracting flu or anything.

Day six. Animals, animals, animals. We're in our stride now so there was really no stopping us. Worked way after hours churning out loads of four-footed, two-footed, hairy, furry, skinny, fat creatures, big ones, small ones, horned ones, hoofed ones. Worked like crazy to get it finished in time for the deadline. Lined them all up and told them to reproduce. You should have seen the glee.

Spent the last hour making what we like to call people. Advanced creatures who use about a tenth of their brain. They possess extraordinary powers and, unlike the other animals, they can crack jokes, arm wrestle, buy and sell used cars, sit around yelling at the TV, punch a hole in the ozone, design and build petrol bombs and fireworks, sit in traffic queues and insult other drivers, and destroy the other species in huge numbers. That said, the exciting thing about all this is that they bear an uncanny resemblance to us. It's like looking in a mirror. Tomorrow, after a late start and a full fried breakfast, I'll go and introduce myself properly.

The reason we were working to such a tight deadline today is that tomorrow we're having a day off.

The bank clerk's back, I've not seen him in here for a good while. He's about eighteen and looks nine. He wears his crisp new suit with pride and tries not to bend his knees too much when he sits down, for fear of generating creases. He has blond hair and oh . . . I don't know . . . facial features. Imagine your favourite eighteen-year-old guy – it could be him. He has a nose, two eyes, a mouth and despite many attempts, no beard. The landlord would ask for ID but it would mean engaging in conversation.

I worked in a bank once. It was back in the days when blond young things like this guy were featured in promotional adverts saying 'It's not all work, work, work, you know' and then you'd see him wander off stiff-legged into the sunset in his crisp new suit, a female bank clerk on his arm.

Those were the days. Nowadays the only job you get for life is sewing mailbags in a category A prison.

Work's a funny business, isn't it? I don't enjoy my job at the moment. Used to. When it was new and brought in more money, and I didn't know if I could really do it, then I loved it. Now it's same old, same old, and I can't recall which bit of the big picture is me, which cog in the machine I am.

I recently heard someone say that we should go back to a six-day week; that a day off is not good 'cause blokes were designed to be fulfilled in their work. I guess I have to admit, when I finish my contractually obligated job, then I get to work on the career I really wish I had.

My black book starts with nothing. A blank canvass. On the face of it God just snapped his fingers, or coughed, or whistled or something and bingo! Things started happening. Light, colour, growth, time, movement. But if it only took a click of God's mouse, then why take seven days? Do the lot in half a morning, break for coffee and go to a villa in Spain for six and a half days. I reckon he made a meal of it. He messed about, made stuff and played with it. Enjoyed it, marvelled at it. Did what we were destined to do with it. He just got in before the rush.

There's a lot of heated debate about God's work. Was it really seven days? What about evolution? What about dinosaurs? And Neolithic men? And morphing apes? Frankly, I couldn't give a monkey's. I know it's irresponsible and I'm the first to bash on about intelligent faith, but I have other concerns. Like what's the point of wasps? And why are puppies designed to remove the wallpaper?

What matters to me is that somebody wired this planet up. Whether it took seven days or seven million light years is not my bag, baby. Whether we're the only planet with life, or just one of hundreds, I don't mind. Can you imagine though, if there is life out there, and if we did colonise Pluto, or Goofy or whatever. Local news wouldn't get a look in, would it?

'Tonight's headlines: Traffic Chaos on Mars as Red Traffic Lights are installed for the first time, another cheese crisis on the Moon, and astro-scientists have discovered a massive crack in Uranus. But first the local news in your area: America wins lots of things, Chinese election founders as polling officials keep losing count, and Australia's hot. Goodnight.'

That groundbreaking story about the cardboard box blowing the wrong way down your local high street wouldn't get a look in.

This universe is plenty big enough for me already.

So, back to work. Not literally, I'm quite happy here, heading for my second guest ale of the evening. There's a local beer fest on and I'm currently enjoying a brew called Maggot's Regurgitation. Sounds like a racehorse actually. But I assure you it doesn't taste like one. I finish it and go to the bar and ask for a half of something going by the name of Blue Cheese and Egg Yolk.

The bank clerk's there, waiting for his Guinness to settle.

'D'you work at the bank?' I ask, the bloomin' obvious being my specialist subject.

He nods cautiously, doesn't look me in the eye.

'I worked in a bank years ago.' I force a laugh. 'Before you were born.'

He raises his eyebrows and wills his pint to clear at twice the normal speed.

'D'you like it?' I ask.

He shrugs. 'It's a job.' And he scuttles away, to a seat much further than the one he was previously inhabiting. I didn't mean to scare him, I was just working on my feminine side. You know, talking.

It's a job . . . I wonder if the Trinity thought that about marsupials. Or slugs. Yeah, if creation was going to get boring I guess slugs would be about the time. It sets me wondering how much job satisfaction exists in the known world at any given moment. Many men fall apart when they have to retire. Their job might be mundane and grim, but it gives them purpose and a reason to get up in the morning. It probably means that even though most men look downright miserable at work, they're really having the time of their lives. Compare it with how animated they look when they're out in Cutter's wining and dining their loved ones and yes . . . that figures.

22. Sin City

Jonah 3

Jonah stands on the beach and prays. There's nothing quite like the threat of death and torture (not in that order) to sharpen your spiritual life. He doesn't know much about these people, but what he does know is all bad. Jonah didn't sign up for this.

When he enrolled in the School of Prophets, there was no talk of lonely abandonment on a blood-soaked beach. Back then it was all words from the Lord and visions from God. There was nothing in the training manual about surviving shipwrecks, storms and fishy stomach acid. Now here he is, stinking of intestinal gas, covered in half digested plankton, cowering on a strange beach in the world's most dangerous country.

The Assyrians relish their tourist trade. They don't have that many visitors so they make the most of any who drop by. They kidnap their enemies, garnish them with flowers, and skin them alive; newcomers get to lie pinned to the ground while living flesh is stripped from their flailing bodies. These are a people who gorge themselves on the suffering of strangers. And Jonah is well aware that he has never been more of a stranger in a strange land.

These people don't deserve good news. They deserve punishment. Swift and painful. Wherever they go they bring rape and suffering, pillage and destruction. They wreck temples and carry off children. They turn free men into slaves and wives into whores. They are a byword for evil.

When you've grown up in the shadow of fear, when you wake every day wondering if bad men will break in and destroy everything that matters to you, what are you supposed to do when the God of heaven tells you to go and condemn the bullies and pronounce judgement on such a fierce people? Oh sure, it's good news if you're not the one who has to do it. It's great if someone else is going to tell them they're about to be fried from on high. But when you're the one wagging the fist and jabbing the finger? When you're the one surrounded by the murderously insane? I don't think so.

Jonah picks up his baggage and moves up the beach. It isn't the luggage he left home with, that was all lost at sea when the reluctant sailors threw him overboard as an aquatic sacrifice. No, this is undigested bits of food gathered from the inside of that great fish. Jonah figures if he is going to die he might as well perish with a full stomach. He'll sauté the few bits of decomposing squid, pan-fry the gangrenous eel morsels and prepare them in a white bile sauce. Then he'll make a final sacrifice to God, send his mum a postcard of Ninevah at night, and go down and tell the locals they're stuffed.

The capital of Assyria is a brutal place, drunks hang out in the gutters, prostitutes flash their thighs in scarlet doorways, wild dogs drool and snap at passers-by and gangs of armed kids torch anything that stands still for too long. As Jonah picks his way through the sea of blood, dog sick and discarded body parts, he feels hopeful for the first time. Maybe, just maybe, this will all have a happy ending. Maybe he'll escape with his life, maybe this will get reported back home, maybe he'll be a hero and get his name on the roll of honour in the School of Prophets, and maybe, just maybe, the Ninevites really will die a slow and agonising death. Bless 'em.

Of course, the unthinkable might happen, Jonah might die screaming, no one will ever know he came, and God will forgive the Ninevites for their history of violence. But he's joking of course. Die he might, but God forgive the Assyrians? Yeah, right. I don't think so. Pork'll grow wings and start tweeting first.

Forty days later, Jonah's sitting slumped on a hill nursing his wounds. Oh, his skin's intact. Apart from a stubbed toe and a broken fingernail, nothing's damaged. The wound is internal. Jonah's in agony because the unthinkable happened.

God's forgiven 120,000 miserable sinners. Murderers, pimps, rapists and slave traders. All forgiven Snap! Just like that. Where's the justice? Where's the hope in a God who won't deliver fire and brimstone when he promises it. Burn 'em! Now! Please! Let's face it. They deserve it. But there's no fire from heaven. There's no earthquake or angels of death. There's just a bunch of sad people, mourning their sins and hoping to start again. And there's a miserable prophet, sitting on a hill, caring more about his own good than the welfare of 100,000 men, women and children.

Oh and there's a pig overhead, flying off into the evil Assyrian sunset.

Yuppie throwback has persisted in coming to Cutter's, even though it must be clear to him now that this is never gonna be Wetherspoons and chicken wings will never feature.

He has jet black hair, a jet black suit, a jet black cell-phone, and jet black rings under his eyes. He spends much of his time in Cutter's on his mobile, talking to the world outside about his world inside. He drinks bottled lager and looks cool but earnest. If I am honest, he scares me. Not in the kind of life-threatening way the *neighbour of the beast* in the pool room scares me. It's the smell of success that follows in his wake. The upwardly mobile aroma. They say that downsizing is the thing now. Pleasing to know I'm trendy at long last.

You see in one sense I can cope more easily with a bruiser like the pool room *neighbour*. He's a known quantity, but yuppie throwback can probably mince my brain and dice my personality with a few quick-fire quips, a couple of sassy put-downs. He'd probably make purée of my faith in the time it takes for me to say 'Hallelujah'.

A friend once told me that he was worried his life was beginning to fragment. There were cracks all over the place. He looked long and hard for God, and couldn't find him. Till he looked in the cracks.

But does a self-sufficient guy like yuppie throwback have any cracks? Common sense tells me he must do, but maybe if they're papered over he won't be able to spot God in there. Maybe I should go over and tell him about all this. You're kidding, right? Me? Go to the coolest guy in Cutter's? Where's the loo?

When I get back there's no sign of him so I shut my eyes, open my Bible and jam in a finger. This is commonly known as seeking guidance, and it's very ill-advised. My finger lands squarely on a question mark. Useful. It's as if God's saying, 'What d'you think you're doing?' I work my way cautiously backwards, like a man teetering on a ledge six floors up, and I find I'm smack in the middle of Jonah. Oh great, so now I'm on my way to Tarshish and God's going to send the *neighbour of the beast* to swallow me up.

You know, Ninevah was a nasty place. A really nasty place. I bet Jonah didn't want to go there because he was absolutely terrified of being kidnapped and tortured. Now this is a book that we often bandy round to encourage people to go out and witness more. But if it's a model for that, first you should enrol in a school of prophets. Then you should find the most dangerous place on the planet, say Colombia, or North Korea, and then set up shop in their local high street with a big sign saying *The end is nigh*. Obviously in Colombian or Korean. It may be worth your while doing a five-year Open University course in the local lingo as well before you go. Oh and one final thing, make sure God's in on the planning, 'cause if he's not, you may as well just jump inside the nearest shark now.

You see, Jonah was skilled and trained in this stuff. He wasn't just your average Joe, sitting behind a computer thinking about tuna sandwiches. He probably regularly stood up in front of people and told them difficult things. He was used to addressing big crowds, and let's face it, 120,000 is a big crowd.

For three days he wandered about Ninevah with his billboard and his flat cap.

'In forty days it'll all be over. Don't pay out good money on any extended guarantees.'

No wonder the poor guy is angry when they don't get barbecued. Not only has he risked his life and all four limbs, not only has he done the one thing he really didn't want to do, he also has to live with the fact that he prophesied and was proved wrong. Ouch. That's a big bruise on your pride Jonah, where d'you get that?

And worst of all – those inhuman monsters down there haven't got what they deserve. Innocent people die every day. But nasty Ninevites? Oh no. That would be unfair.

Having visited the Cambodian killing fields and S-21, the brutal interrogation centre of the Khmer Rouge, I was later given a newspaper article about a man called Comrade Duch. Duch was the head of the Khmer Rouge special branch, and commander of S-21, formerly Tuol Sleng High School. The article had been written by Nic Dunlop, a journalist who spent years trying to track down Duch. When he finally found Duch, in a plastic-covered shack in the district of Samlot, he discovered a man who had found God; a man deeply sorry for his crimes.

I read this with mixed feelings. Here is a man who orchestrated thousands of killings. Many innocent people died in the most horrific ways. He ordered the killings of children as well as men and women. There are thousands of photographs of those who died under Comrade Duch and the other heads of Tuol Sleng. There were only seven known survivors from that appalling prison.

Of course, it's really nothing to do with me. It's none of my business. But like Jonah I can sit under a tree and complain about injustice.

The grace of God seems naïve. Why should tyrants and torturers be forgiven?

Thinking about this puts me off my beer. I push it away and some of it spills across the table. It really was a terrible day when we visited that prison. I've never felt so scared and wretched.

But I really have to leave it with God. I can't work it out. He has to.

The last thing I want to be is glib, either about the evil of men, or the grace of God.

Perhaps all we can take from this is that God really, really doesn't want to destroy what he's made. As bad as people can become, it's alien to him to want to wipe them out if there is any other way. And maybe too it gives us a glimpse of the massive power of the cross of Christ.

If Ninevah can be forgiven, if I can be forgiven, if Duch can be forgiven . . . There's hope.

23. Show Me the Money

Luke 16:1–13

Felix sits at his desk and stares out of the grey window. Everything's grey this morning. The sky, the sidewalk, the people on it, the future they're looking at. Unless Felix can pull something out of the hat his life's over. He'll be pushing up daisies. So what can he do?

Whistlin' Dixie pokes her head in the door.

'Cawfee?' she chirps at him, her lipstick setting her mouth in a permanent smile.

'No thanks, Dixie. Not now.'

'Revolver Jack just called up. Wanted to pay that fifty grand he owes the boss. I told him to come round.'

And she's off, whistlin' as she goes. Good old Dixie, he'll miss her when he's gone. So Jack's coming round, eh? Why not pocket the fifty and make off into the sunset? There are worse things he could do. He's being fired anyway, might as well just take the money and run. Only then he'd be out there alone with fifty grand in his pocket and Revolver Jack on his back. No job and no safe place to hide. That won't do.

He swivels in his seat and stares up at the pinboard behind his desk. Snap after snap of successful cases. Telulah Stash, Johnny Swag, Mike Machete. He'd served 'em all well and they were all on the books, owing the boss a pretty sum between them.

Now there's a thought. If he could get them on his side, make a few friends out there, maybe he wouldn't end up in the gutter at the end of the day.

Felix isn't even sure why he is being fired. Someone pumping dirty rumours into the boss's head about him. It doesn't come down to much more than that. And before you can say, 'Here's looking at you, kid,' he's out on his ear. Packing his bags and serving out his time. By five tonight he'll be jobless and roofless. A tap comes on the door. It's Dixie.

'Jack's here to see you, Felix.'

'Show him in, Dixie.' Felix checks himself in the mirror, and gets in to character. 'Jack! Jack! Good to see ya. Pull up a chair, fancy a bourbon?'

Jack's a big guy, barrel chest and beef for legs. He doesn't often look happy but today he may just leave with a smile on his face.

'Jack, you know that fifty grand?'

'Got it right here, Felix.' He pats his chest.

'Easy, Jack. You may not need it all, keep space in your pocket for some of it. You know, I think you just need to pay back twenty-five.'

'Twenty-five?'

'Yeah, we're feeling generous. Make it twenty-five grand. Celebrate, throw a party for your employees. Get in some dancing girls and a fancy cake.'

Jack does leave smiling. And Felix sits staring at half the money, wondering if he's done the right thing.

The phone rings. Dixie's dulcet tones waft in from the other office.

'Felix! It's Stiletto Sam!'

Felix picks up the phone. 'Sam! Sam! How you doing? How's the leg? They can do great things these days, Sam. How much you owe us for now? Oh just make it twenty. Really. I ain't kidding ya, Sam. Come over, drink some whisky and let's chat.'

Sam likes whisky and drinks a lot of it so this one takes a little time. But the outcome's the same. A small pile of notes and a sunbeaming customer. Just by coincidence, Johnny drops by with Mike straight after, and the two of them are quickly sorted. These guys are like Laurel and Hardy – Mike's the straight guy and Johnny keeps falling over things. So when Felix offers his discount there's a right old hey-ho between the two, Johnny's all for taking it but Mike's not so sure. They dance around each other for a while and Johnny manages to chuck bourbon over Felix, Mike and the money. When he pulls out a fat cigar and lights up, Felix is a mite worried everything will go up in smoke. But eventually it all calms down and they go their merry ways.

When they're gone and it's quiet Felix picks up the phone and calls Telulah. She always gets his pulse racing and it's tempting to just cancel her debt right out, but then she wouldn't need to come round paying him a visit. And he still wants the visit . . .

Twenty minutes later she's a vision of beauty right there in his office.

'OK, Mr Fricker, tell me the deal here. Word is you're doing the dirty on the boss.'

Telulah leans back in her seat as she talks. Her crossed legs go on forever and a Chesterfield hangs from the corner of her dark red lips; sassy grey smoke snakes toward the ceiling. Felix licks his lips.

'Telulah, I . . .'

'Don't flannel me Felix. What's going down here? I hears you're packing bags. Up and outta here with the trash can. So what's all this Mr Niceguy-Freemoney? You acting under orders?' She leans forward and blows a smoke ring. 'Or just your own steam?'

'It's true. I'm history here, kiddo. Lady, I gotta do something or I'm rat food.'

Telulah, nods, smiles and stubs out a lot of remaining Chesterfield. Then she smoothes a hand down her endless thigh and pulls a Beretta.

'Don't mess with me, Fricker. I owe Twenty thousand dollars. Who do you think the boss is gonna come looking for when there's only ten in his pocket tomorrow? You want that I end up pretty in a ditch?'

Felix is on his feet, hands out in front of him, trying to calm things down here.

'Look, Telulah . . .'

'Hi Felix, you want more bourbon? Oh!' The door flies open and the gun goes off. A bullet slams into Dixie's shoulder. It spins her round and she catches her head on the door frame. Her mouth is still smiling as she slumps to the floor.

Felix moves to catch her but Telulah's up and training the gun back on him.

'Stay back, sweet boy, let the big girls deal with this. You OK, Dixie?'

Of course she's not OK. She's out cold.

'Telulah, just go. Forget the deal, pay the boss in full. What do I care?'

'Felix! I'm asking you nicely. Siddown and stay put.' She crouches over Dixie, pulls a silk handkerchief from nowhere and pads up the entry wound. 'OK, she'll live, call the hospital.'

Felix dials and the ambulance is on its way. While they wait Telulah lays the gun on the desk between the piles of notes.

'So this ain't no scam?'

'No. Telulah, I'm in trouble, when the boss kicks me out I have nowhere to go. This is the only thing I know. So I figure, if I can use his money to make a few friends out there, what's the problem? I'm gonna need friends this time tomorrow. Sure the boss ain't gonna like it, but I'll take that chance.'

A siren wails outside and an ambulance draws up. Telulah holsters the gun and moves to the door.

'OK, sweet boy,' she purrs, 'I guess I have to play ball now. Tell Dixie I'm sorry, and I'll send round an errand boy to pay my half tonight.'

She turns to leave, then stops and looks back, her bright green eyes flashing as she says, 'Oh, and come up and see me when you're homeless. There's a side door at the speakeasy. Slip up the stairs after midnight and give a low whistle. You do know how to whistle, don't you?'

Felix nods. He knows all right, though right now his lips are way too dry.

There's a sweepstake going on in Cutter's. Someone's cottoned on to the old scam of showing pre-recorded horse races and getting the punters to bet on them. Stacey's going round taking bets and chirping happily so it's probably her idea. She's wearing a low-cut top to distract the guys from the logic of what they're doing. It's working.

She smiles at me but I can see there's not much hope in her eyes.

'I s'pose you're not into gambling much? It's only a flutter.'

Now why would I not be into gambling much?

'Well you know, you being religious and all . . . By the way, I went to a christening recently.'

How does she know I'm religious? I've never told a soul. I don't come in here wielding my little black book like an axe, or going round with a shaking tin demanding money for Christian Aid. Do they all know? How do they all know? You won't catch me in a T-shirt that says,

Jesus loves you, but I'm his favourite. In fact today I'm wearing the rather more worldly: *I feel much better now that I've given up all hope . . .*

'Yeah, and I do believe there's something in it, but the thought of going to church puts me off, and I wouldn't know where to start with all this Jesus loves you stuff . . .'

Sorry? I realise she's been giving me a window of opportunity for the last two minutes.

'Oh well, never mind eh? Maybe next time?' And she's gone.

Why does it always happen like that? Why do the best chances to talk about your faith always crop up when you're distracted by something else?

And how do they know I'm a Christian? It doesn't matter, you just missed a key witnessing moment, mate. Oh, brilliant . . . I have, haven't I . . .

I shut up quick as I realise I'm turning into Gollum/Smeagol. Oh great. I'm mad *and* a lousy Christian.

Quick, let's think about something else. Sweepstakes. Money. Fast cash. I flip to Luke. This strange parable Jesus tells about the guy who saves his own neck by using his ex-bosses money. What's going on there? Be shrewd, use your cash to benefit others and to make friends. And if you do, you'll get extra bonus points in heaven. It's not exactly 'love they neighbour' stuff, is it? Elsewhere there's a rich fool who just stores up his dosh for himself. That kills him. Maybe this is something to do with using money rather than abusing it. Even though it's the boss's money that the manager is wafting about willy-nilly, the boss still seems impressed that the guy makes a good fist of it.

There's an old saying that goes something like: God made things to be used and people to be loved. And we got the two mixed up. Along with things like, *There's a*

God-shaped hole in all of us – you won't find it in the Bible. Jesus never actually said it. But maybe that's what he's alluding to here. One thing's for sure, he's not saying be as poor as you possibly can. OK, he talked about us having treasure in heaven (see Lk. 12:33) and we've got to put God before material desires (see Lk. 14:33) – Jesus even told one guy to sell everything and give it away. (And that clearly hit the spot 'cause the poor guy was well miffed.) But we've got to be wise where money's concerned.

This tale of the unexpected is swiftly followed by another macabre story (Lk. 16:19–31). Stinking rich Dives abuses poverty stricken Lazarus and then ends up roasting in hell. While he's being slowly sautéed he has a discussion with father Abraham (nothing to do with the Smurfs as far as I can glean) about how he can get a message to his brothers concerning the appalling nature of the afterlife down below.

So, is this a tale about money, or a tale about salvation? Despite the fact that his extremities are being pan-fried, Dives still seems to want to laud it over poor Lazarus. Basically he's an evil toad. Lazarus is now happily in heaven, regularly winning *Who Wants to Be a Millionaire* and eating junk food all day. And there's no way he's coming over the Grand Canyon to mop Dives' brow, thank very much. Once you're dead there's a great divide and there's no chair-lift, or paragliding allowed.

So do all poor people go to heaven? Probably not. Is Dives in the hot and bother because he was rich? I doubt it. In life he had no redeeming qualities. And in Jesus' gripping tale he wasn't redeemed. We need more information here. That's the snag with the little black book. You can't just pick'n'mix. You've got to take the bulk order. You can't just base your life's philosophy on one thing Jesus said.

It's the same with anyone. Take one single comment of mine and use it out of context and you'll be able to prove beyond any reasonable doubt that I'm a misogynistic, war-mongering, bunny-hating Buddhist. Take another phrase and you could convince the world I'm a woman. It's that easy. But read the whole of this book and the truth will stand out like an intelligent man in parliament. It'll be undeniable – I'm a misogynistic, war-mongering, bunny-hating Buddhist.

Jesus shuts the door on this particular parable with a question about reliability. If you can't be trusted with the meagre wealth you've got down here, and all earthly wealth is apparently nothing compared to that place where the streets are paved with gold, how can you be trusted with heavenly riches? How you use your money indicates whether you can be trusted with anything of great value.

Ouch. That hurts.

24. Talking from Balaam's Ass

Numbers 22

Balaam stands and watches the clouds of dust. He lives in a shack surrounded by red earth so he always knows when people are coming to visit because their horses kick up enough smog to drown a small village. No one ever walks to see him; they'd be dead before they got halfway, the terrain is too inhospitable. There are no wells between here and anywhere else.

Balaam is a good man, but lately he's grown weary of his isolation. He's wondering if there's more to life than seeing the future and talking about it. He'd like to live it a little before he dies.

He watches the clouds move closer; he figures he has another half-hour yet. He'll take a bath and get his servant Melchior to knock up some food. He doesn't often wash, there's no real need to. Melchior has no sense of smell and who else is going to care?

He even digs out his one clean tunic, though it's not as clean as he remembers it. And there's a hole in one of the seams. Never mind, it'll do. Doubtless these visitors haven't come to see him for some fashion advice. He doesn't go out to greet them, it's not his way. More fitting for an old prophet to sit in a wonky old chair in the shadows, his face veiled by the darkness. And most importantly this vantage point allows him to see them before they see him.

The men dismount and veil their eyes from the burning sun. There are four of them – three heavily armed. It's the usual kind of delegation. One of them spots the thin figure rocking on the lopsided porch.

'Hello! We're looking for Balaam, son of Beor. Is this his place?'

Balaam doesn't reply, instead the canvas over the doorway flaps and Melchior appears carrying a tray of warm wine.

'You've found the place you're looking for, gentlemen. Balaam will see you up here.'

If they haven't found what they're looking for, they're way off course. There's nothing else round here for a hundred miles.

The unarmed one is clearly the leader. He has dark wild hair, running down his back like a mane. He walks like a king and looks you straight in the eye. His right cheek is peppered with small scars, as if a rock once exploded too near his face. He's the only one who climbs the veranda steps, the others stand in a triangle, hands on swords, ready to defend. Balaam can't think what on earth they're expecting, unless they fear Melchior is a god in old man's clothing.

'Are you Balaam, son of Beor?'

The leader still can't see his face. It's a neat trick Balaam plays on everyone. Until he stands up his features won't be clear.

'I am. Who's asking?'

'My Lord is King Balak of the Moabites. He requests your assistance.'

'And your name?'

'Morak.' The man clicks his heels and bows a little. Not too much though.

'Go on,' says Balaam.

Melchior offers the wine and the man scoops up the cup without looking at it. He knocks back the drink in one tip of the cup and wipes his mouth with the back of his hand.

'A strange nation has invaded our territory. Tales of death and destruction accompany them. My king fears that they will wipe us all out and steal our land. This is no small request. My king is strong, but these savages have already devoured the Amorites.'

'Well, I'm no warrior. I can barely urinate in a straight line. And I doubt if Melchior's much use to you, he's got no teeth and less strength.'

The man smiles. 'My Lord Balaam, we know you're a seer. All we want you to do is come and place a curse on these people. If you do, they won't succeed and we'll drive them back.'

Balaam stands for the first time. He's smaller than they expected. His face is like that of a small bird, he has quick furtive eyes, and a jabbing head.

'So you know I'm a seer, eh?'

'Your reputation travels.'

'It would have to, living out here in the middle of nowhere.' Balaam stretches and yawns. 'Oh, I'm getting too old for long distance travelling . . .'

'We have the proper payment.'

Morak snaps his fingers. One of the others returns to his horse and unloads a saddlebag. The thing is bulging.

'That's not straw in there. It's gold.'

Balaam's little eyes grow to twice their bird-like size. All pretence of mystique forgotten, he leaps up and bounds down the steps to the horses.

Morak's horse is a beauty; it's a former racehorse, fed and trained for war. Balaam walks around it, biting his lip and smoothing his hand across the flank. He only has a donkey. A stupid ass that never does what he says.

'We know that if you bless a nation they'll prosper, likewise if you curse them they're doomed. It's just a simple thing we ask. Kelor, show him the bag.'

One of the other men flips open the saddlebag. The gold inside winks at Balaam. It's tempting . . . very tempting.

'Stay here tonight,' he says, 'we have food, and Melchior can make you up some beds.'

Oh really? Melchior raises an eyebrow and sighs audibly.

'I can curse people till the jackals come home, it only works if my Master commands it.'

Morak looks around for another shack. 'Your Master?'

Balaam's still stroking the sleek white champion. 'Yes,' he says, his mind elsewhere, 'my Master.'

The men suck their way through a rancid meal of maggoty bread and elderly stew, and then spend a sleepless night on lice-infested straw. They see little of Balaam until the early hours of the morning, when he arrives unannounced and hovers over the bleary men.

'The answer's no,' he says, clearly angered by the answer he has to give.

And then he's gone. Melchior gives them some stale bread for the journey and they find the horses saddled and watered and ready to go. The gold is untouched and Balaam does not wave them off.

Three days later they're back. Balaam's heart skips a beat when he sees the familiar clouds of dust.

'My Lord Balaam, King Balak is insistent. He needs you. Without your curse on these people we will fail. Balak will give you anything you ask. Gold, spices, linen, concubines. He is a wealthy man and you clearly . . . are not. We can change all that.'

Morak stands beside his white racehorse. This time he has brought twenty men with him – all finely dressed, all at Balaam's mercy. Balaam wonders if the horse is on offer.

Morak looks at the ground.

'Everything is on offer,' he says, sadly.

So the men stay one more night, though this time they have brought their own food and bedding and they choose to sleep around a fire under the stars. They stay up until late, muttering in low voices and passing around a sweet-smelling pipe.

In the morning Balaam greets them with a smile and a lot of gleeful hand-rubbing.

'My Master says I can come,' he says, 'when do we leave?'

The officials ride on ahead. Melchior and Morak keep pace with Balaam and his ailing donkey. In the burning sun, it's slow going but thoughts of gold and racehorses keep Balaam set on course.

At noon, they shelter beneath an overhanging rock and eat some of Morak's food.

When they begin again the donkey plays hard to get. He jumps a ridge and scoots across a field. It takes a while to bring him back in line. When he does this a second, then a third time Balaam starts to lose his cool.

'Come on, you stupid ass! I've got a job to do.'

'You're a dead man.'

The three men freeze.

'Is it me?' says Morak, 'Or did your donkey just speak?'

'You bet I just spoke. He's a dead man, and if you two schmucks don't sidestep a little you'll all be pushing up the daisies.'

There's no denying it. The voice definitely seems to be coming from his donkey. If it's ventriloquism, the lip-synching is perfect.

'Is this something he often does?'

'Are you guys stupid?' the donkey quips. 'Step aside and let the angel through.'

'What angel?'

'The masterblaster with the fiery sword. 'Cause Balaam's history.'

'Me?'

'Oh, don't come the innocent. You knew the Boss didn't want you going with these losers. So why d'you go back and ask him a second time?'

'He said I could come.'

'Sure he did. But only because he was tired of you asking. It's curtains now, mate. End of show. You knew his answer the first time. Any last requests? 'Cause you got an appointment with death.'

The rain hacks at the windows like 1,000 killer bees. It's practically coming down horizontally. I stand at the kitchen window and stare hard at it. I wanted to go to Cutter's tonight but the weather ambushed me. So my wife's gone out to see a few mates and I'm stuck inside on a babysitting shift. The rain makes me feel strangely nostalgic; I always used to love watching it attack the windows during boring lessons at college. So I regress back to my college menu and make some thick white toast and open a cheap can of beer. It has minus 5 per cent alcohol content.

Then I do what all single people up and down the country are doing. I stand and eat over the sink. The rain still sounds like a load of jabbing fingers, drumming at the window. I turn to my book and find a strange tale of talking animals and killer cherubs. I read. I chew. I think.

So let's get this straight. God sanctions Balaam's trip, then pulls the plug and leaves him alone with a somewhat vengeful angel of the Lord. What's going on there?

I mean, let's be fair. Balaam asked and got permission.

I flip to the tiny book of Jude. There's a clue here. Balaam's name crops up all over my little black book. For a strange prophet who's famous for his talking animal he certainly gets about.

Snuck away in Jude there's a passing reference to this Dr Dolittle character, and like Judas, he's remembered for his bad points. 'Like Balaam, they will do anything for money.'

Ah, that'll be it then.

Why does Balaam bother to go back to God for a second opinion? He knows what God has said: 'Don't do it.' Which bit of *No* doesn't he understand? Nothing's changed. Or rather, only one thing's changed – the size of the prize on offer. Balaam can name his price now. He can have anything he wants. All he has to do is come and diss the Israelites. A few short sentences and he's a rich man.

Balaam doesn't persist in prayer for any good reason, he intercedes for himself, and the new house he has in mind. So presumably in heaven at the daily board meeting God says, 'This guy's on at me again. I thought we made it clear. I don't want him badmouthing my guys.'

And that's the point where the angel offers to deal with the problem.

So God says, 'OK, Balaam, you go if you want. But you'll find my answer's still the same. And as of now, you've outstayed your welcome.'

Enter this pesky talking donkey. Shrek isn't the only one with mouthy mule trouble.

This dumb animal breaks its silence and saves the day. Well, it saves it for Balaam. It's less satisfying for others.

The Moabites and Midianites are a *little* disappointed because they come joint second in a battle where winning is the only reason for taking part.

You see, he still goes. But following his chat with the mighty angel, instead of cursing the Israelites, Balaam blesses them. You can imagine the panic in Chez Balak when that news breaks. Balak was looking forward to a cosy one-sided fight. Instead he's ushered in a grim future of fire and brimstone, toil and trouble for his own people. Crushed skulls and cracked foreheads are the best they can look forward to now.

So, what did we learn here today? In an age of talking computers and plastic light-sabres is there anything relevant in this strange showdown?

Well, first the bloomin' obvious – don't be greedy and if you fear you have been, always take a donkey with you on long journeys.

Secondly, Balaam set out on the wide road, but still found one final slip road just as he was on the brink of Death Valley. And, although this was never the best course of action, the God of heaven still found a way to use it for his purposes. Maybe there is no absolute plan. Maybe life is often a series of dubious decisions which the Boss then has to turn to the good. Maybe you think you've messed up and you've passed the last escape exit. Look again, there may be another one along soon.

And finally, don't be fooled into thinking angels are just sweet choirboys.

25. The Evil That Men Do

Genesis 18 and 19

It's another hot day in the desert. Another few miles on the clock.

But it's no ordinary day.

God drops in on Abraham, bringing Gabriel Bond and Michael Leiter with him. They're on their way to annihilate Sodom and Gomorrah. Primarily they want to remind Abe that he's under contract – not unlike any of us guys who get excited about following God into the unknown, then get all panicky 'cause we've just *followed God into the unknown!!* But they happen to mention in the conversation that the lush, fertile Jordan Valley, is toast. And now we see another side of the divine personality. Not only the intention to eradicate the miserable self-serving lot in Wickedville but also the – wow! – ability for God to *change his mind!*

Abraham has mixed feelings over his Lot. Not his lot, his nephew Lot. The boy ventures out with him, strikes out in search of freedom, only to give up halfway and settle down in a nice little retirement home in Badtown.

But Abe can't give up the boy, like so many parents with so many prodigals, Abe is still waiting, still hoping all will be well with the next generation. So his heart sinks to his boots when he hears of the imminent apocalypse. His mouth dries up and his stomach kicks bile into his throat. He hears a voice screaming in his head: 'Don't do this, don't rain down fire on an innocent man. Lot may be stupid, he may be wayward, he may be morbidly curious enough to want to live in Sick City, but he's not a bad person. He's family. He can't die screaming with his flesh melting and his face on fire. That's not justice.'

So he says: 'If there's fifty law-abiding citizens in Sodom – you wouldn't nuke it, would you? It's not in your nature.'

A pause.

The celestial hitmen shuffle their feet and unbutton their black suits. One of them removes his shades and polishes the lenses. They look at their Boss.

'No. Not if there's fifty.'

They strut on. Abe follows, grabs a bulky shoulder, pulls them back.

'What about forty-five? Forty? Surely not if there's forty?'

Another awkward silence. Gabriel rubs his brow, the other one coughs.

'No, not if there's forty.'

They move off but Abe holds on, stops their progress.

'And what about thirty?'

It's getting embarrassing now. And dangerous. These guys don't mess about. Suffering fools gladly is not on their 'To Do' list. Abe's a stranger in a strange land. Who's gonna miss him? They're hardly going to stick up a 'missing person' poster with his face on it.

Abraham swallows, the taste of bile still lingering in his throat.

'What if there's only twenty . . . Or even ten . . .'

The assassins look at their Boss, exchange glances . . . imperceptible nods pass between them. It's as if they knew Abe would be difficult about this.

'OK. If there are ten righteous people we won't destroy the place. Enough now.'

And so the deal is struck, Abraham lets go of the suit and the three men move off, God in one direction, the two hitmen in the other, down towards Sodom, down to the place where death will soon rain from the sky.

But there's no sudden retribution here; the guys are intent on finding out if the rumours are true. Giving the benefit of the doubt does feature on their list. There's a slap-up meal with Lot; the guy entertains angels unawares, so there's still some good in him, then. Things are looking up for Sodom. After all, it's not that far back that the wicked of the world got washed away in the father of all floods. Surely it can't make sense to wipe out another generation, after all it's not as if . . .

There's a knock at the door. The hitmen are just putting on their jet black pyjamas, fitting their Rayban eyeshades. Everyone freezes. This is bad. Very bad. There are a lot of voices outside, and they're all male. Many of them drunk. Lot pulls on his dressing gown, throws nervous glances at the two assassins.

'It'll be all right, I'll get rid of 'em, just a few revellers turned out of the pubs . . .'

He puts the night chain across the door before he opens it a little.

'We saw you had visitors, we'd like to meet 'em. . .'

'Not now guys, it's late. Tomorrow.'

Lot pushes on the door but a colossal rock of a hand slams against the wood.

'That's not very polite. I think you should invite us in.'

'Don't be stupid, there's too many of you.'

'Then send 'em out. We've got a party organised for them.'

'Please. Don't do this. These are good men.'

'We'll decide about that. Come on, you stinking son of a . . . open this door.'

More fists rain down on the wood. Lot's family appears. He has two beautiful daughters and a gorgeous wife. They cower in the corner and look very small. Lot looks at his two daughters and his heart breaks. He knows there may be a way to buy time.

He sighs, and then fumbles with the door chain; the movement is hard because his hand's shaking so badly. Somehow he opens it, slips outside and pulls it shut behind him. He catches his breath when he sees how many men are out there and what state they're in. This is worse, much worse than he imagined. He's sometimes had nightmares, nightmares where the neighbourhood breaks into his house at midnight and rapes his entire family. The dreams are gruesome; he always wakes with a sick feeling in his stomach and a headache that lasts all day. Now he's standing here about to make the prophecy come true. He wilts visibly as he speaks.

'My daughters are young and beautiful, very beautiful. Why don't I bring them out for you? they'll satisfy you . . .'

The men aren't here to bargain. They're here to satisfy their twisted, ugly desire.

'Who the ---- d'you think you are to tell us what to do? Forget your ------- daughters – we'll have you!'

Their language is as cruel as their intentions. The air around Lot turns a bruised purple as a hundred perverts spill out their gleeful filth. Lot swallows and stares. He says nothing, and for a moment there's nothing but a tortured silence.

Then there's a sudden sickening cheer and the men rush for Lot. Fists grab at his clothes and begin to rip them from his body, a stray hand jerks his arm and begins to twist it behind his back, another pulls at his hair. There are teeth tearing at his neck. Lot screams. And in an instant it's over.

'What the . . .'

'Where's he gone?'

'I can't see a ------- thing!'

'---- me – I'm blind!'

With a snap of the fingers, or a twinkle of the eyes, or whatever, the hitmen call time on the corruption. They start with the eyes, always the first port of call when sin comes around. Most things that corrupt and discredit us begin with a lingering gaze.

The men are blinded, Lot is pulled to safety and it's as good as over. While the city delinquents wander about like zombies, clawing at the night, the angels give Lot his final instructions. Like the grizzly end to an Agatha Christie play, they gather the family in the drawing room. Lot, his wife, two daughters (thankfully intact) and their fiancées. By my count that's six. Six is not enough. Six is four below ten. Time's up for Sodom. The fun is over.

They flee. The sun comes up. The fire comes down. The people pay dearly. Charred bodies litter the streets. The sickening putrid smell hangs in the air for days, weeks, afterwards.

The hitmen came in peace, they were looking for a get-out clause. There was none. The angels brought a rope and the men of Sodom have kindly hung themselves on it. Good riddance.

Just one problem – I hope those two never come knocking at my door and start rifling through my closet. There'd be more skeletons than in the streets of Gomorrah.

The airwaves have been full of sour news today. Sometimes it feels like I slip into Cutter's in a haze of doom. Bad news gnats buzz around my head, nipping at my brain, gorging themselves on the little bits of hope I have stored up there.

Stacey and Brian's girlfriend are at the bar, chinwagging about this and that and all those other things men don't understand. Being in my bloody-minded, the-world-is-a-bad-place frame of mind I decide to tell a joke to two complete strangers. Never a good idea.

'You know why men and women can't have a short conversation?'

The two women stare at me, hopeful that this intrusion will soon end. Stacey shakes her head and says a surly, 'No.'

'Because women don't understand the word "short" and men don't understand the word "conversation".'

The audible hilarity this conjures up is not dissimilar to the sound of one hand clapping.

'I'll have a pint of that please,' I say, reverting back to type.

All credit to them, in spite of my ugly intrusion, they quite happily return to their chatting and know precisely where they had got to in their discussion. As Stacey pulls the pint she starts on about church. Apparently she's recently been godmother to her friend's daughter Britney.

'So I had to answer all these questions and I'm supposed to say yes and I'm thinking, no! And there's all these people watching. Do you renounce evil? No. Do you know Christ's love? No. Do you confess your sins . . .

I think I've got the picture. Inside my guts twist as if someone's wringing the juice out of them. Part of me feels aggrieved as if Stacey's wiping her shoes on my best shirt. But at the same time I have sympathy because I know this scene, I've seen it played out a thousand times. These poor outsiders who don't know a Bible from a computer manual are made to stand up in front of a bemused congregation and asked to repeat lines which may as well be in Aramaic as far as they're concerned. Brain's girlfriend laughs and nods and sympathises. I take my beer and run – Remembering in the nick of time to pay for it.

I don't really want to sit and submerge myself in rape and violence but my eyes fall on that particular passage and morbid curiosity keeps me reading. The thing is, it's like something off TV. Fact *and* fiction.

Sodom and Gomorrah. The town which gave it's name to a formerly illegal practice. Why did the Gomorrahites get off so lightly? No one tells that annoying lager lout who's relieving himself in your rhododendrons to Gom off, do they? How come? You don't call your PC a gomming thing when it crashes yet again. Why?

This is a lurid and shocking tale. Lot has the pick of the local cities to find a des res and ends up setting up his stall in a town that's one big red light district. A town living on borrowed time. How much bad luck is that?

Things must have looked up for a short while when he started entertaining angels unawares. Not for long though. And when it started to go Pete Tong it went very Pete Tong indeed.

You evil piece of low-life, Lot; you nasty, weak-minded, cowardly piece of low-life. How dare you offer those girls? How dare you? The men out there have come for their own kind, the least you could do is offer yourself!

In my mind's eye, I can see the torches, the leering, twisted faces, the seething aberration of humanity. And it scares me. Even as I rant in my head and pass judgement on this cornered rabbit of a man, I know that I'm afraid too, afraid it might happen to me someday, and more, afraid that I would do exactly the same thing.

Poor Lot. Poor me. Poor, poor girls. They even have fiancées. What about them? Where are they in all this?

Hang on. I falter for a moment, rusty brown brain slowly kicking into a higher gear. Haven't I seen this story somewhere else? Sounds strangely familiar. I let my fingers do the walking and flip ahead, past the decades, through the centuries, like some biblical Marty McFly, eventually landing up in Judges 19. Some old geezer turns up in a village where a couple of travellers are sitting in the town square, looking for all the world like a couple of *The Big Issue* vendors.

'Don't stay out here,' he says, 'whatever you do. Come home with me . . .'

Turns out the couple have come from Bethlehem, the guy's been chasing after his wayward wife slash concubine – the text seems unclear – either way she ran off back to her father and he wants her back. After a convoluted few days, a knife-edge thriller of a week, will they/won't they pack the donkey and head home tonight . . . they eventually pack up and make tracks, only to wind up in the Biblical equivalent of the Bronx. The three go to the old man's cosy nook, relax, party and chill out. Then there's a knock at the door. Surprise surprise, the local ruffians are demanding that the old guy send out the stranger, not the girl, oh no – the man. What is it with these people? Any strange dude in town is greeted with a kind word and an offer of rape. Once again the genial host stands on his doorstep, a frail barricade between the wolves and the lambs. He stands there shifting from foot to foot, once again offering a beloved daughter in place of a total stranger. Hospitality clearly means a lot to these people.

The story is oh so familiar except for one vital thing – there are no celestial hitmen in town, no divine Terminators to blind the local thugs and torch the town. This is sin central and if the visitor is to escape – then his wife must take the rap. In a chilling denouement I witness him pushing her outside, pulling the old guy to safety and the men of the town spending the rest of the dark hours abusing her repeatedly for sport. This place is hell, this is every occupied town, in every war, in every century. This is the Russian villages ripped open by invading Nazis, this is vanquished Germany at the mercy of vengeful Russian Cossacks. This is Pol Pot's Cambodia, Idi Amin's Uganda, Mussolini's Italy, Saddam's Iraq, Pinochet's Chile, and in far too many places, Britain's Empire. This is every persecuted town, every defenceless minority, every cornered priest, every ruined monk and nun, every helpless child held up for mockery, butchery and scorn.

This is not the happy side of the Bible. This is the hard stuff. This is gritty, sinful reality. The raw, seeping, maggot-ridden, gangrenous wound that still chews away at humanity. The serpentine lie that we could be like God and do whatever we jolly well like.

These are people with their own children and families and mothers, who walk out the door of an evening just so that they can desecrate other people's children and families and mothers.

'Back in a couple of hours dear, have the bath water ready so I can wash away the blood and bodily fluids, I'd hate to have to do that in lukewarm water . . .'

I get up. I have to. If I read too much of this stuff it makes me seethe, makes me spit fury, makes me want to go out and kill someone. The Good Book's not supposed to make you want to be so bad. Surely.

I cross the room, ask for another pint.

The reason this is cutting so deep is that the papers are full of corruption and violence. There's one brutal case that detectives are calling the worst they've ever seen.

When so many Jews lived through so much misery in the thirties and forties, it's said that this was only possible because local, ordinary people complied. Not all of them, not all by a long shot. But many.

There's a bully inside of all of us, isn't there? We all seem to start off OK, politicians, teachers, lawyers, accountants, but somewhere along the way we come to a junction and the wide road seems to be the obvious choice. Actually choice is too strong a word, choice suggests that it's an even fifty/fifty, this way or that, right or left, but most times I've strutted down that open road for a good half a mile before I realise that I'm actually on it.

We ask people to renounce evil and repent of sin. We give them the words and the instructions, but not the ability or understanding.

I stay in Cutter's a long time, long after my second pint has gone warm.

I want to stay in this haven, I don't want to go outside and face the seething mass of humanity. There may not be an angel to fry the bad guys for me.

I'm scared, too much bad news drives out my courage, steals my faith in human nature. One news story about an abducted child and I'm convinced my street is full of abductors. I know the Bible's full of good guys, I know the planet is too, but right now all I can see are the bad ones.

And the ugly.

26. The Creator and the Call Girl

Ezekiel 16

He picks up the DVD, prizes open the case – the catch is always stiff – and removes the disc. There is no writing on it, no label. He depresses the button and the tray opens. He places the disc inside, crouches in front of the television and watches. There's no menu, it just begins to play immediately. The scene is a field. The sun is rising. A ragged refugee appears over the horizon. She's carrying a bundle of bloodstained clothes, her last few possessions in the world. Her face is lined with tears and worry, there is blood caked on her hands and feet. She limps heavily after a searing night of nothing but pain.

He fast-forwards a little then presses 'play' again.

The figure stands in the field now, looking around for an appropriate spot. Over in the corner will do. In the shelter of the hedge. She squats down, scoops a little earth to make a dip in the soil, then lowers her bundle of clothes into it. She stands up, takes one last look at her lost treasure and stumbles away, sobbing silently as she goes.

The sun continues to rise and the bundle starts to move. It's not a collection of clothes. It's a new baby, on the first – and maybe the last – day of its life. It cries and kicks and throws off some of the rags. Its strong lungs bellow for milk, the little thing is growing impatient.

Footsteps approach, heavy feet crunching in the dry earth. A giant of a man stands over the child and stares at it. What on earth is this in his field? He was about to start ploughing; he'd have mashed the child into the ground.

The baby stops screaming and lies still for a moment. There is blood smeared on its face and an umbilical cord trails out of the wrapping. It's still smeared in its mother's fluids. This baby has never seen water or soap. Even animals get licked clean – this child is filthy.

The farmer scoops up the bundle and the baby screams. He ignores the cries and scrapes off the afterbirth and the globs of drying blood. He takes it to a nearby trough. The water's freezing so he dips a bucket, and carries everything to a fire in the nearby forest. He throws on a few more branches and sets the metal bucket down in the flames. When the water's warm he takes handfuls and smears them over the child. The baby stares and screams alternately, it's hungry really, and a clean body will not satisfy this craving for milk. When the child is cleaner he wraps it in his own cloak. Finally, he get round to food. He fishes in his bag for a flask of milk, forms a makeshift teat from some torn strips of cloth and shoves it in the child's mouth. The forest falls quiet. The baby sucks and after an eternity, falls asleep.

He fast-forwards ten years.

The child's a little girl now, running with her foster dad. Covered in filth once again, only this time it's from playing in the mud and looking after the animals. He runs the disc on further. She's thirteen, fifteen, seventeen. With every passing glimpse she looks more beautiful. The farmer sells a field to buy her the best clothes and make-up, jewellery and perfumes. He pays to get her the best hair fashion and skincare.

He pauses the film on her eighteenth birthday.

She's looking radiant. No muck on her face or stains on her clothes now. She's perfect. She's happy. If only this were the end of the film. He lets it play on. The girl turns away from the camera, kisses her father and slips out of the farmhouse. The camera follows her away from the field, through the forest and into the town. She's in the bar now, laughing and joking with the local guys. She's enjoying herself, laughing and joking with them. They buy her drinks and she swaps kisses with them. One of them invites her home, so she hands the barman her necklace for the drinks and follows him. The others come too.

The man runs this on. He doesn't particularly want to see her dancing naked for these guys, doesn't want to watch her hand over her rings and jewellery for one night of sex. Especially a night that will set a clock ticking in her body. She wakes the next morning alone and cold. She gathers up her clothes – some of them got ripped in the frenzied activity. She can't find any of the men she met last night. The bar's closed and silent. She wanders home, back to the farmhouse, wondering how she will explain what she's lost.

Six months later and she's ill. The men took more than her virginity. They took her life. She's dying. It'll be a long time before the disease kills her, but the date is set.

The farmer looks after her, sells another field to buy drugs, makes her food and helps her through each day. At night, while she sleeps, the farmer sits up for long hours, staring at the field outside, remembering how he found her and gave her life.

God freezes this last image, staring at himself on the TV screen. This has happened to him so many times. And he guesses it will happen again. Time after time after time. He will go on, forever rescuing people and watching them growing up to abuse him. There's a cry outside his window. He turns to catch site of another fleeing refugee and another bundle tucked in the dip beside the hedge. He sighs and stands up, but at the same time his heart skips a beat. Here we go again . . .

Back at Cutter's, Builder Brian and his fiancée Katrina have fallen out. (I finally eavesdropped on the right conversation and found out her name.) They hate each other now, they can't stand the sight of one another, there are death threats in the air and it's conceivable they may never pass the time of day or share saliva again. Strangely they're both in the same bar in the same pub, not six feet from one another.

He's with his old pal, knocking back the pints and waxing lyrical about the delights of singleness. (Not quite in those words.) She's bought a friend for emotional strength, moral support and so that she can talk loudly to her about the appalling nature of her ex's body, mind and strength. In that order. He can hear but is pretending he doesn't give a flying fag end. I know this because he has his own volume button up to 11.

The air's so full of venom it seems quite clear to the rest of us. They're hooked and will soon be hitched. They're expending so much energy on expressing their hatred – it has to be love. They're clearly very concerned that it might really be the end. And that would be devastating.

The rest of us stand back and watch. They could have sold tickets. The last act of the circus is a foregone conclusion, of course. There'll be a passionate reunion and the promise of undying love – if they don't kill each other first. And that's the bit that's interesting. There'll be spitting, swearing and whole lot more lurid details before we get to the never-ending love scene.

I blot out the live entertainment for a second and flick open the leather-bound oracle. There's a good fire roaring in the grate and I decide it's a good day for sex and violence.

Abandoned children kicking about in their own blood, naked women lying in a field, a prostitute who pays to sleep with as many customers as possible? This isn't exactly sweet Corinthian love, or gentle Galatian fruit, is it? But then neither is Daniel in the lion's den, or David hacking off Goliath's head. They never were U-rated stories, we just put pretty pictures to them and made them that way.

Yet in amongst the violence and the lurid behaviour, there's another story. One that runs all the way from the Garden of Eden to the New Jerusalem. God's a lover. He can't help it.

When Daniel sees an angel by the River Tigris, his reaction is one of terror. He falls to his knees grovelling before the God of heaven. But the next thing he feels is not a light-sabre splitting his skull, but a firm hand on his shoulder, and a voice telling him there's no need to fear, 'cause God loves him.

When I screw up yet again – when I find myself covered in filth and slithering around in those prodigal pig faeces, full of self-loathing and self-pity – the things I fear most are God's judgement and God's rejection. I have this idea that he'll hate me now. 'That's it. You were tolerable for a while, mate – but now you've done that? Get out. End of story. Get down the God Centre – find yourself a new saviour.'

What I never really consider is the pain and the jealousy I might have caused.

Philip Yancey, in his incisive book, *Disappointment with God*,[1] points out that there are two strong images of God in the Old Testament. The caring parent and the jealous lover. We sing about the parent all the time; there aren't many songs about the jealous guy.

Ezekiel 16 isn't the only story God tells about his painful love affair with humankind. A few chapters down the line the rejection occurs again. This time with two sisters, Oholah and Oholibah, two more names which really should catch on again. They both end up as enthusiastic prostitutes, avidly throwing themselves across the beds of every good-looking young superstar. It's clear from the story he tells that the pain for God is intolerable at times.

Hosea's entire book is dedicated to the same theme. His entire life is, too, as he ends up marrying a wayward woman, just so he can demonstrate how painful it is for God to live with people who are always falling for other lovers.

Seems to me the message is simple. God just wants to love and be loved in return. Shocking, ain't it? If someone said that of me I'd feel compromised. It's true, but I don't want you to know it's true.

'Ah, you know what Dave's like, he just wants to be loved . . .'

I wonder if God didn't actually spend the first few hundred years of life in a holiday home on planet Earth, just so that he could hang around with Adam and Eve, rubbing shoulders, chatting, laughing, swapping stories and seeing the sights. It's hardly likely that he made people and then said, 'Bye, then – see you at the flood.'

I think of my dad; my dear, kind, gentle father. The kind of guy people describe as a real gentleman. And he is. He really is. And sinful as he is, he's knows how to give good gifts to me and my brothers. He's a chip off the old block. And God knows I'm lucky to have that. I'm blessed to have a dad who shines a light on the Creator for me, a guy who gives me a glimpse of my bigger Dad.

The sparks have finished flying. The fireworks are over. People are wandering home, awed by the quality of the entertainment. As predicted, Katrina and Brian are in each others arms, not at each others throats, which did look likely at one point. The wedding's back on, as long as he can remember which lay-by he was in when he hurled the ring out of the window.

And if I skip to the end of this story I find the same. The prostitute finds herself back in the arms of the lover she'll never have to pay. He's holding her close, stroking her hair and telling her it'll be OK. She's been a fool, she's embarrassed herself and him. But he can't reject her. He can't slam the door and lock it forever. It's not in his nature.

No sooner has he's vented his grief, no sooner has he stomped about and broken a few bits of crockery, than he's back out on the streets looking for her. A prodigal father, he leaves the safety of home to go tramping the city streets for some sign of life. Knocking on all the doors, flicking through the telephone directory, asking after all the wayward guys she'll be chasing. And the moment he finds her, he can't help himself. He wants her back. He's besotted. What else can he do? What else is he going to do with that storehouse of good things he's got saved up? Every box has her name on it.

'Come home, come back. I'm not standing here with a loaded gun. I've been angry, sure, but my anger's gone. I don't want to live without you, come home and let's start doing some real living. These lovers may look tasty, but their hearts are cold, their lives are empty.

'Come back and let's start again . . .'

---

[1] Philip Yancey, *Disappointment with God* (Grand Rapids: Zondervan, 1992).

27. Ezekiel's Dung

Ezekiel 4:9–17

This is the end. Ezekiel's had a hard enough week. He's been trapped in his house with his tongue feeling like a doorstop and his mouth all gummed up. People think he's had some nasty viral thing, that's left him hoarse. If only that were true. Ezekiel would give his right arm to just have a virus, except that he can't as he now has to lie on it for a year and three weeks.

And now this. It's not easy being a prophet. It's never been easy.

But this is the pits . . .

His guts aren't good at the moment anyway, what with that terrifying vision the other day . . . So now he's staring at his own pile of dung, while that familiar voice in his head is whispering about drying it out. Oh great, what's this for? So he can put it in a glass case and hang it on the wall? Or better still, stick it on string and wear it round his neck.

'Nothing so strange Ezekiel, just cook your food on it for the next thirteen months.'

'What? You're kidding, right? It's a joke, yeah? *Please* say it's a joke.'

'Ezekiel, it's simple. Make up some barley bread mix, stick it in a jar and then just lie on your side for a year and bake the bread on smoking human excrement. What's the problem?'

'What's the problem? What's the problem? Have you forgotten about a little book called Leviticus? You wrote it! It spent twelve weeks at the top of the *Israeli Times* Best Seller's List. Quoting from page 37, "A priest should not defile himself . . ." I think you'll find that what you're asking me to do is enough to ban me for life. What will it prove anyway?'

'Israel will eat defiled bread in an exiled land.'

'Well, hey, I've got a great idea, I'll tell them that. I'll announce it through a megaphone. I'll graffiti it on every wall. I'll release a record, make a movie about it. Post it on the Internet . . .'

'Ezekiel, just lie down and set fire to your faeces. I mean, what else are you going to do with it? You can't get up and bury it.'

'Lord, please, don't make me do this. It's not holy, it's not spiritual. I'll lose my job. I'll be a laughing stock. And I'll smell terrible.'

Silence from heaven. Ezekiel looks round. Is he alone? Has God gone? He shivers a little. A cold wind whistles round, tumbleweed blows past him. Is that it then? Has he lost his job? Was all that Technicolor stuff by the river just a big show? Is he an ex-prophet? Was he not really up to the job? He shuffles from one foot to the other, scratches the back of his neck nervously. Ho hum. Perhaps he'll go and find a good book to read . . . Not Leviticus, that's for sure. Maybe he'll . . .

'All right, Ezekiel. You win.'

Ezekiel breathes a sigh of relief. He collapses in the dirt and hangs his head. He hears the sound of lumbering hooves.

'See that cow over there?'

Ezekiel knows where this one's going.

'I'll bring the cow along each day, it'll leave you a nice warm present and you can use that.'

'Thank you. Er, God . . . Are we still friends?'
'Do you really need to ask?'

There's a huge pile of canine excrement on the front step of Cutter's. Looks like a Rottweiler passed by. And not too long ago . . . It's still steaming. So far, no one's been caught in this succulent brown mantrap. But it'll happen. Sooner or later, someone'll place a brand new gleaming white trainer smack in the centre of this foul-smelling monstrosity; especially after a couple of pints in the pub. I try not to dwell on the thought and move inside. It's a regular day. I order my pint. The landlord's daughter is serving but she's off on another planet and doesn't notice my winning smile. I contemplate warning her about the unpleasant mound on the doorstep but can't quite find the words – plus I don't want to appear too anal (no pun intended) on the cleanliness front. Instead I settle down with Ezekiel. Oh great. More excrement.

Ezekiel's prophetic career didn't begin like this. It started with visions and four-faced flying creatures – eagles and lions and burning coals and honeyed scrolls. That was awesome, that was grand. That was quite clearly holy.

Now look at him, discussing his own bodily waste with God. Where's the holiness in that? Why can't he just tell cheeky parables and wise sayings? He never even wanted to be a prophet anyway. He went to college to be a priest, not some weird seer. He just got up one day, stood by the river, and the heavens opened. There was no rain, instead wind and fire came storming out of the north, carrying winged creatures and the voice of God.

So, God breaks his own laws. Hmm, interesting – that's not supposed to happen. There's a great long list of banned substances and illegal practices that make a priest unclean, including visiting prostitutes, sacrificing children, emitting semen and being found in possession of crusty scabs, ripe boils and crushed testicles. Priests have to be bloomin' careful you know; the number of regulations these days is staggering. You only have to burp and you're in quarantine for seven days. You don't only have to do the right thing, you have to be seen to be doing the right thing. Otherwise it's 'grab a rock and let's have a stoning'.

In the end it's God who repents, not Ezekiel. God's clearly the more humble of the two. God relents and Ezekiel goes off with a saucepan to wait at the business end of a cow. But he must have been well shaken by the episode. Apparently communicating with people is far more important than his own rules and regulations. Getting through to them matters more than getting it right. God's using shock tactics, prepared to go much further than Ezekiel to get his point across.

How often do I sit here in Cutter's and miss the piles of dung lying around? Stepping gingerly over them, often avoiding them altogether because they can't possibly be of God. The God of heaven uses nice clean things to communicate, not smelly old flyblown human excrement. Doesn't he?

Seems not. Seems he's irresponsible. Seems he'll use anything. The dangers of not getting through to people are too great. All means must be employed. Savoury or not.

Ezekiel's off to the barber's tomorrow.

'Highlights for you sir? A mullet perhaps, or layers? Short back and sides, then?'

'Nope. Just take the whole lot off.'

'But you're a priest, sir.'

Even though the old law says priests can't shave their head – God says it's a good idea.

'Would you like to keep your sideburns, sir?'

'Please.'

'I'll put 'em in the bag along with the rest of it.'

28. Party On

Revelation 21:1–7

John wakes to another long day. He's old now, too old for this. He's lonely and spends each day with fear in his belly. He has many memories which keep him going, but it's not easy. Those days of parables and parties seem a million years ago. He wanders around a little, finds some water, splashes his face and takes a drink. Then he remembers. It's Sunday. God's day. He kneels and talks to the man he once used to lean on. Hundreds of images assault his brain; for some reason his head is more alive than ever. He hasn't eaten anything but his brain is suddenly agile. He recalls his friend on that mountain, glazed in eye-burning white. He sees him bend to scoop mud and smear it across dull eyes. He sees him dodging stones from an angry crowd, he sees him masked in blood and open wounds. And he sees him by the water, cooking fish and chatting to his other best mate.

Oh, why does he bother? He's just torturing himself. Jesus isn't coming back. At least not in his lifetime. He'll be long dead before the earth has fresh divine footprints on it. John'll never see him again. Not in this life. John searches beneath a boulder just outside his shack. He pulls out a few scraps of scroll, precious letters he's kept over the years, food to keep his soul alive. He reads them yet again, mouthing the words quietly, and the words become prayers and the prayers become tears. A son of thunder? John? Not any more.

And that's when he hears the voice. So loud the trees shiver and the ground shakes. It's like a hundred horns blaring. He turns and sees and falls on his face.

'John, it's me. I am the Alpha and Omega. Everything begins and ends with me. Now, concentrate. I have a lot to show you, write down everything you see . . .'

A gleaming figure stands in front of him surrounded by lights and lampstands, he's not unlike the one John saw on that mountain all those years ago. John squints, shuts his eyes, wonders if he's hallucinating. He's not, this is real life. The man's face is like the sun, his tunic's full of gold and white and it shines like a new dawn. In his left hand there are keys and the metal sheds searing sparks. In his right there are seven stars, and his eyes blaze like a furnace. John shades his eyes but keeps staring all the same.

The daylight fades and above them both an epic begins to play. Dragons and demons come tearing out of the darkness, there's blood and gore and fire. The world twists and turns as the hordes of hell vie for supremacy. There are prostitutes and horsemen, plagues and famine. On and on the battle rages. John scoops up his pages and begins to sketch and scribble. Somehow he finds space for it all. At first he planned to merely log it in his brain for later, but he knows he'll never remember all this. Bowls of wrath pour out like an ocean of fire. Heroes and villains ride this surf while puppet kings rise and fall. He doesn't understand what he sees, but he keeps writing, he can't stop. It could be minutes, hours, days or weeks, he has no idea how long this story lasts. All he knows is that when the sky falls silent, he's exhausted.

Then, before he's had time to draw breath, a final curtain pulls back and the last chapter begins. He grabs his pen and writes again, his hands cramped and arthritic.

Then I saw a new heaven and a new earth, for the old heaven and the old earth had disappeared completely. And the sea was gone too. And I saw the holy city, the new Jerusalem, coming down from God out of heaven looking beautiful, she was perfect, like a bride looks as she walks down the aisle.

I jumped as I heard a loud shout. I looked up and saw a mighty throne – the figure sitting on it looked as brilliant as gemstones, like jasper and carnelian. An emerald glow circled him like a rainbow. And from the throne came flashes of lightning and the rumbles of thunder. And in front of him were seven lampstands with their burning flames twisting up to the sky.

'Look,' said the voice, 'God is finally moving in. He is making his home here, with his people! He will live with them forever, and they will always be together. God himself will be right here, in the same neighbourhood. He will take away all of their sorrows, and there will be no more death or sadness or crying or pain. For the old world and its evils are gone forever.'

And the one sitting on the throne said, 'Look, everything is new! I'm giving you a new start.' And then he said to me, 'Make sure you get all this down, for what I'm telling you is all trustworthy and true.'

And for the second time in my life I heard him say, 'It is finished!'

And I knelt and sobbed.

He lifted my head, steadied my shoulder and said, 'I am the Alpha and the Omega – the Beginning and the End. I will give the water of life to everyone who is thirsty and there'll be no charge! It's absolutely free. Keep persevering, keep going to the end and you will inherit all these blessings, and I will be your God, and you will be my children. This is a cast-iron promise. If you're thirsty, don't hang back, bring a bucket and get to the water of life.'

(Based on Rev. 21 vv 1-7, NLT)

There's a party going on in Cutter's. Apparently it's Brian and Katrina's official engagement do, they had one a while ago but as they had a bust-up and got back together, they thought it was worth another do. Two Boys in a Mood are on stage doing their punk version of 'Don't Cry For Me Argentina'. Apparently Swimming in Sewage are waiting in the wings for their moment of glory. There are a lot of people here tonight and everyone coming through the door is offered a glass of beer and a wafer of engagement cake. Even me. I feel embarrassed but somehow warm inside to be offered a part in it all. Blond bank clerk's here with blonde girl bank clerk on his arm, also child-repellent teacher and his partner. Brian turns out to have an awful lot of builder mates, especially as there's free beer. Edgar's in with one of his sons. Only Yuppie Throwback is missing. Oh, and genial Steve of course. Swimming in Sewage offer their breakneck rendition of 'Bob the Builder', (Brian's lot love this) then it's over to DJ Radiotherapy who plays a selection of seventies' and eighties' unforgettable classics.

I, meanwhile, hook out my book and venture into the party of all parties: Revelation.

It's big screen stuff, this. I can see John now, lying on his back, watching the future play out like *Star Wars* Episode 10. Plagues and storms, dragons and wild horses come hurtling out of the sky towards him like that giant intergalactic juke box at the end of *Close Encounters*. For a guy who never went to a multiplex in his life it must have been terrifying. They say that audiences fled when they first saw an approaching train on the big screen; well, John saw many more awesome special effects than that. I'm surprised he didn't have a cardiac event. Although you could argue that he did.

Locusts, moonblood, revolution and rage all feature in this action adventure (director's cut), and ten hours and a massive body count later we reach the denouement, a fitting climax involving trumpets, angels and a city of gold.

The red carpet rolls out and you're the star of the show. You look around to see who's getting the applause and the accolades – but it's you. That was your life, mate, welcome to paradise.

There's not exactly an exhaustive description of heaven in the Bible. There's a list here of what there *won't* be. But not a huge amount about what there *will* be. I don't know about you but I sometimes sweat about my entrance ticket. Three o'clock in the morning is often a really good time to wake up and stress helplessly about whether you're going to make it, and whether you'll like it if you do.

One thing's for sure, I don't want to end up in the other place, on the toasting fork just right of Dives. That was my main criteria for throwing myself on the mercy of the God of heaven in the first place – I was terrified of the thought of going down in the celestial lift rather than up. It was three years after that that I discovered God was actually interested in this scummy Baldrick of a person going by the name of me. My faith had been founded on sheer terror; took me a long while to make it down the high street to the cash point of grace.

It's just guesswork but instinct tells me it's gotta be good up there, and all this notion of singing back-to-back choruses for ever and a day doesn't cut it for me. I want thrills and spills, I want a place where I can ride rollercoasters, eat chocolate, be brilliant at football, watch movies that aren't predictable, tell jokes that make everyone laugh and generally just be happy with who I am. I want to dance like Travolta, cook like Floyd, sing like Elvis, look like Maximus and paint like Rolf. As opposed to real life where I dance like Maximus, sing like Floyd, look like Rolf, paint like Travolta and cook like Elvis. I guess I've decided that life must be a pale reflection of the afterlife. What we know and love down here, can only get better. Life's too short for so many things because it's just the taster. The hors d'oeuvre, the matchpot, the free sample you get before you buy.

Guilt and fear will be old money, currency that lost its value years ago. There will be singing, in tune and out of tune, there'll be break-dancing, ballroom dancing, bad dancing, round your handbag dancing and obviously – the Macarena. And I'll be able to keep up. No one will ever be untrendy, bad hair will be in, so will long hair and short hair, and grey hair and no hair. It'll all be cool. There'll be no hoovers or toilet ducks or ironing boards, and washing up won't mysteriously appear from nowhere and stay piled up precariously like a sky-scraper for three days. Cockroaches will be cute, wasps won't sting, dogs won't bark and children won't whine. And all those odd socks will be reunited with their loved ones. The air will be clean and the cars emission free. Flatulence will smell like the Lynx effect and junk food will be really good for you. There'll always be something brilliant on telly – on all four million channels – and the remote will never fall down the back of the sofa. Batteries won't run out and light bulbs won't go at two in the morning while you're sitting on the toilet. There'll always be enough loo paper too.

Every joke will be funny, even the cheesy ones you get in sermons. Although there won't be any sermons, of course. You can eat and never get fat, drink and never get a beer gut. You'll never lose your keys, never pay tax, never feel old and always be in the right place at the right time.

Life will go on and on and on.

But it'll never get boring.

I feel a hand on my shoulder and jump out of my skin. I look up. It's Adam the teacher.

'Can I get you a drink?' he asks.

Things are going so well, even us blokes are communicating with one another. Though I have to admit I'm a bit tongue-tied.

'Er . . . yeah . . . thanks . . . a pint of Guinness, no er . . . Kronenbourg.' Kronenbourg? I hate lager.

He's back and places the drink down for me.

'Party's going well,' I say. 'Great dancing.'

'I don't dance much.'

'No, me neither.'

'I wanted to say – thanks for chatting that time. Hope I didn't seem a complete moron. I'd had a few too many, you know.'

'No problem. I was glad to be . . . er . . . glad. I was glad.'

'You're always on your own reading that book.'

'I am, aren't I?'

A pause. He's waiting to see if I can actually string a sentence together.

'OK, it's erm . . . you know. The Bible.' (These last two words said very fast.) 'I come here to get away from it all and . . . get my head straight.'

'So you're religious?'

I nod, almost imperceptibly.

'My girlfriend is too,' he says.

'Really?'

'Yeah, she reads her horoscope regularly and does all that feng shui stuff. She's been to church a few times. I won't go. My dad was into it all, but we never saw him. He was never home.'

'He was always at church?'

'Yeah, he was one of those . . . oh, what do you call them? You know . . . er . . . lay readers.'

'Ah. Right.'

'Not all clergy are bad. Not saying that.'

'Sure. Have a seat, by the way.'

He sits.

Not a lot more happens for a while. We watch people dancing quite badly. Funny thing is, we look cool but they look a lot happier.

He's looking at my leather-bound book again.

'Ever read it?' I ask.

He snaps his fingers. 'Little bloke killed Goliath . . . Daniel.'

'David.'

'Yeah, David. And the bloke on the cross of course. You know why it's so hard to read? All that begatting. What's that all about. He begat her, she begat him. Where's the point?'

'Well, begatting's quite enjoyable when you think about it.' I shrug. 'I know it's hard but I think it makes a lot of sense if someone can help you understand it. There's a lot of normal people in here, it's compiled in a style that's . . .'

'Like reading the telephone directory.' He snaps his fingers again. 'Narnia. *The Lion, the Witch and the Wardrobe*. That's in there, isn't it?'

'Er . . . kind of. Actually that's C.S. Lewis trying to help people into it a bit more.'

His girlfriend waves from across the room. He's up pretty quick.

'Well, nice talking to you.'
'Thanks for the drink.'
'Oh, that's OK. See you again sometime.'
'Enjoy the dancing.'
He laughs. 'Thanks.'

I'm left musing on my black book.

Why is it so hard to read? How come there's so much good stuff packed in here, but it's so hard to piece together?

John had the same problem of course. He saw a vision of a world he couldn't understand, a future he couldn't fathom. So he scribbled it down as best he could.

Perhaps that's why the Bible's so hard. It's a collection of writing about a world of which we know so little. A strange hinterland where the Creator interacts with his creation, the one outside time keeps stepping into time. It's a bit like trying to get your goldfish to fit a new hard drive, or change the gearbox. Doesn't compute. We get glimpses and one-liners, clues and a few footprints. But it's hard work. We're following a trail here, a line of crumbs that will lead us back to the One who once gave us a banquet.

I guess one day, when the trumpet sounds and the city gates are thrown open, and there's all kinds of razzmatazz, we'll follow that trail to its end and stumble through an open door to find ourselves in a stunning new city. One where there'll be no need for clues and crumbs, 'cause the table will be right there, groaning under the weight of the food, and we won't have to wade through all the begatting. Life will make sense at last.